WHO CONNECTS YOUR DOTS?

THE POWER OF CRITICAL THINKING

Jill Fandrich, PharmD

ISBN 979-8-88851-670-6 (Paperback)
ISBN 979-8-88851-672-0 (Hardcover)
ISBN 979-8-88851-671-3 (Digital)

Covenant Books
11661 Hwy 707
Murrells Inlet, SC 29576
www.covenantbooks.com

CONTENTS

INTRODUCTION

How do you interpret information? How do you digest the content you absorb from news sources today? Were you there to verify the facts? What about information presented online or in a book? How do you know if the information is *really* true? Do you have any "inside" connections to verify the content? Or are you like the rest of us—trying to find some way to "connect the dots"? What do you know about *critical thinking*?

One day I listened to a story from a particular news source. It was almost fascinating to witness how emotionally charged one reporter had been while delivering her message and how passionate she was that only *her* version of the story was the "right" one. She was even visibly upset with anyone who expressed an opposing view. I then selected an alternate station and watched a different reporter share the same story with similar heartfelt concern but from an opposing viewpoint, conveying *his* version as the only "accurate" one. He also became outwardly agitated at the sounds of someone opposing his view. Each reporter displayed zeal just as comparably intensive as the other, and each was also deemed believable, yet they had clearly secured opposing positions. *How can this be?* Two separate stations, two different reporters, the same topic, yet completely opposing views while both claimed to be factual. I repeated this process many times with random stations, and the results were consistent. There were opposing positions, and each one "passionately" professed to be the accurate one. So, *who is right?*

I will admit, there was a time before this when I chose a stance, almost simply because it was what I had *wanted* to be the right story. I found myself caught up in the frenzy and emotion of it all, which was not hard to do! The eye-opener for me occurred as my firm, definitive, infallible, 100 percent right, no-way-can-it-ever-be-wrong stance was—well—*wrong!* I admit it; it was wrong. *I was wrong.* I was "shell-shocked" and had to *scramble* to get all the "egg" off my face. I don't like to be wrong. I don't think anyone *likes* to be wrong. Once I finally acknowledged my error, I asked myself, "Now what?"

Being analytical, my first line of action was to bring myself to an awareness of what was happening around me. I took a step back to collect information and assess the situation. What essentially happened was that I began to *critically think* about what was occurring "out there" in society. This led me to ask question after question, seeking to find honest, substantial answers. I realized that the only *logical* answer lies in the ability to *critically think* about everything of importance.

A lack of *proper* thinking has crept into our society. I have experienced this, as mentioned previously, which has shown me the need to bring forth a book such as this. What if you could begin to listen to any source of news, hear what is being said without a preconceived bias, and consider the information without becoming emotionally charged or passionate about being *right*? Then listen to an opposing view with the same unprejudiced stature all *before* formulating an opinion or drawing a conclusion.

Whatever your reasons for seeking additional information, this book will give you the tools and insight needed to significantly improve your ability to decipher content without emotion, discern truth from "nontruth" with confidence and candor, and increase your ability to handle any situation with a logically based conclusion. Critical thinking is a means to expand the *way* you think, open your mind to new thoughts and perspectives, increase the probability of uncovering factual information, and reduce the volatile impact fed from news media outlets.

I have discovered a need to return to the basics of *thought processing.* The most challenging problem that we all face, quite possibly, is dealing with the people around us, whether it is within your work setting, traffic, your neighborhood, or even within your own home! There is always a need to develop finesse, compassion, and especially the fine art of *getting along* with other people in everyday interactions.

In preparation for writing this book, I studied news sources and observed actions and reactions. I read numerous articles and books and even attended an in-depth study regarding critical thinking, human behavior, and responses. I questioned rational professionals and not-so-sensical ones as well! With each topic, I visualized situations relevant to each one and how they could be applied to professional and personal settings. I also extrapolated key findings from my experience from both my professional career and personal encounters. I organized the information in such a way that would be applicable from numerous perspectives. When applied, these skills and strategies will always prove to be effective, insightful, and *thought-altering*.

Relationships are the most important things in our lives. It is logical to focus a significant amount of time and energy on understanding the nature of people and how our actions affect them. It should be an instinct to show love, kindness, and compassion in every interaction that occurs throughout our days, no matter whom we may come into contact with. Notice I didn't say it would be easy! It is important to display *tolerance* as you listen to opposing views and value the *person* even if you disagree with their content. Learn how *not* to be sensitized by a different perspective. And just as important as it is to have finesse and charisma in our *inter*actions, we must also display the qualities of compassion and tolerance in the *physical* actions we perform as well.

This book is interactive and meant to *educate, inform,* and *instruct*. Within each chapter, you will be brought to an awareness of particular content. You will be challenged to actively participate as you gradually yet consistently develop critical thinking skills. This book explores skills that will refine you as a logical thinker and decision-maker. We look at admirable qualities that will set you apart, illuminate your current skills, and allow you to justify a position as a rational thinker. Read or listen to each section slowly and deliberately yet with vigor and passion while underlining, highlighting, and jotting down notes about key points you want to incorporate into your thought processes and improve your skills. While it may not be applicable to try these suggestions in every interaction, read or listen repeatedly to each section in order to program the information into your mind so you can access these "files" when the opportunity presents itself. Return and refer to these pages frequently, and even visualize the suggestions playing out in your own setting. Think about them often and imagine different outcomes each time.

Ask yourself the following:

- *How could I have applied critical thinking to my interactions today?*
- *What mistakes did I make?*
- *How can I do it differently next time?*
- *Where could I improve?*
- *What did I do right?*
- *What have I learned from this experience?*

Journal your results, whether they are "in progress" or are already successes. Be sure to enter the dates of each entry; be specific regarding the interaction, what questions you asked, how you researched and collected data, and how you reached a logical decision. Include what you did or did not like about your interaction. For your convenience, there is an example *journal* section at the back of this book and a list of suggested *critical thinking questions*. Each may be replicated for your convenience. Review your journal weekly during the first year, then at least monthly, to monitor your progress, reveal how you are growing in the process, and form a lifelong *habit* of logical thinking.

To understand the dire need to train your mind to think this way, you will also be introduced to definitions, acts, applicable books paralleling current circumstances, and much more! By internalizing this information, you are sure to "imprint" inclusive thinking and successful traits into your mind's programming. While this is an enormous undertaking, learning about and truly understanding each of these chapters will undoubtedly grow you as a person and launch you into a decisive leader. Perhaps embrace one chapter per week and study it extensively. Understand what it means, the intent of the content, thoughts, methods, and reasons from the lists provided. Take time to answer the critical thinking questions listed. Visualize your own scenario with each question. Follow up with the concluding "reflect" points at the end of each chapter. Spend time on each one and decipher how you will incorporate this information into your professional, social, and personal life. You will begin to notice logical thinking being displayed more and more naturally in all of your interactions. Ask the same questions as previously mentioned, and journal on how you turned emotionally charged information into a well-processed and logical conclusion, all while maintaining personal and professional relationships. Take the bias, emotions, and unwarranted opinions out of the situation. And finally, after the last chapter has been processed, start back at the beginning!

These methods will allow you to get the most out of this book. Whether you are a leader in the professional sector, an administrator within an organization, head of your household, an online student, or are in a homeschool setting, this book will masterfully remind you of the love, kindness, respect, compassion, *common sense*, and *tolerance* you should build into the very nature of your being and display throughout every interaction.

Let the journey begin!

CHAPTER 1

Who Connects Your Dots?

What is meant by the words *"who connects your dots"*? Quite simply, *who* is influencing your thoughts, actions, and responses? Who is the most influential person or source of information in your life? Do you draw upon content projected from news outlets, social media, Big Pharma, or the Internet without question? Or do you consider the source, where it came from, whether or not bias is involved, what and whom it represents, and who is funding it, then think for yourself? There was a time when the media was *called out* and reprimanded if the stories they presented contained false implications to the slightest degree. Currently, however, there is no consequence for *misinformation*. As a matter of fact, misinformation is now actually *approved and encouraged*. Yes, misinformation is now permitted in our media culture and has existed for quite some time. Most major news outlets are derived from the *same* common source, owned by the *same* company or proprietor, and produce and portray the *same* deceptive content, with the goal of infiltrating, manipulating, propagating, or even inculcating people with tainted data based on "their agenda" of what they want you to know, believe, think, and how to react. *Follow the money.*

Knowing this, it is imperative to bring yourself to an *awareness* of this same operation that is occurring. Begin to ask yourself questions. Who owns each of the news stations? What is their common link or links? Where is the source of information coming from? How might the message be skewed? Understand that you were not actually on location to know if this event really occurred or if the words spoken are valid. You do not have any proof of the expressed content. Are you allowing *them* to "connect the dots" for you, and are you accepting what they say as true and accurate? Or will you listen with an open mind, consider the content and source, view opposing stations or vantage points, and derive your own conclusion? How can you find out more information to substantiate the provided subject matter? Is it possible that there might be other versions of the story? Or could the story have possibly been altered to fit a scenario? How can you incorporate this insight into your analysis when evaluating the other information? It is now imperative to consider all of these things.

From the moment you were born, other people have been programming your mind with *their* opinions, viewpoints, processes, and slews of other information. Your parents or guardians who raised you have shared their version of data, which was embedded into your mind. You absorbed additional information from teachers, friends, television, newspapers, media, social media, the Internet, books, and hundreds of other third-party sources. Other than what you personally have experienced, all of this data input has been presented to you with little to no evidence of truth to support or substantiate it. How often do you actually think for yourself? Did you already realize that other sources have preprogrammed the multitude of your thoughts? Does this knowledge come as a surprise? Or did you understand this concept already? Are your automatic responses to situations in line with what you believe in? Do you even know *what* you believe in? What are your thoughts about *reprogramming* your mind to align with your values?

In what ways do you educate yourself? How about your children or other loved ones? Do you listen to the *worldview* and conform to what *they* think, say, and conclude? Do they have your personal best interests at heart? Be particular about the sources of education, and discover *who* wrote the books, constructed the YouTube, or is teaching the course, and know *what* they stand for and, possibly, who is funding them. It is becoming increasingly transparent that certain major and influential universities have taken an evident and distinctive *political* stance rather than providing unbiased, factual, historical, and educational content. Find the basis for their viewpoint, how and why they select the particular content, and how their conclusions are derived. What do they desire to achieve? It has also become apparent that precious children have become the ultimate source and target for initiating change in this world. If society can program children with the thoughts and ideation *they* want to provoke, rather than relying on the teachings of home and family values, the culture will begin to be, in essence, "brainwashed" to think and respond in the same ways desired and designed by the society or the controlling governing body. Without realizing it, your ability to think freely and undefiled is gradually being compromised and quashed through various and even intricate modalities.

Can you see evidence of bias presented in the news sources? What appears to be the underlying theme? Observe several different and opposing stations. Take some time to analyze your own thoughts regarding the content, the approach, and the viewpoint. Then compare and contrast the similarities and differences you discovered through your analysis. What have you noticed? What is your go-to news source? Are you able to *objectively* watch different sources and uncover dramatically different vantage points and opinions of the same story or event? Take a step back and consider what you have revealed. Do any that you have observed present objective and factual stories from an unbiased perspective, intending to inform you of proven details while allowing you to come to *your own* conclusion? My point here is not to provoke you to pick one side over another and follow blindly but rather to consider both or all sides and realize how the intent is quite often to *manipulate* you into taking *a* side. You are an intelligent person with the ability to think for yourself. You were born with a moral code and have an innate sense of right and wrong. Now more than any other time in history, you are *losing* the same freedom and individuality your ancestors fought hard to provide. While it appeared gradual and subtle for decades, it is now *bluntly* apparent and exponentially driven that your freedom is being reframed with manipulation, brainwashing, and herd mentality.

Ways your freedom is being purloined

1. *News media outlets.* It is quite difficult to deny that nearly all news sources are biased in one way or another. Understand that each one has <u>its</u> own agenda. Consider what that agenda may be, and use your own moral code to interpret the content. Bias generally intends to persuade, manipulate, deceive, or even brainwash. Research whom they are funded by. The media no longer follows a code of ethics in presenting true and unbiased facts. *Know this* as you read or listen to the content of any news source. Ask yourself who is submitting this information. What seems to be the reason for this portrayal or vantage point? What is the desired end result of the story? How could this change? Who will benefit from this viewpoint? Does the source appear to have an agenda? Do they appear to be ignoring, overlooking, or leaving out information in an attempt to sway the viewers? Find a news source with an opposing view. Follow through the same questions and assessment without prejudice and discover who funds them. Are they censoring anyone with an opposing viewpoint? Evaluate the information objectively and draw your own conclusions. Make a conscious effort to gather as much information as possible before jumping to a conclusion. What information is most important? Evaluate the information you collected. What do you think is going on?

2. *Removing your history.* History *is* what it is. What would the point be to ignore it and pretend it didn't happen? That will not change the fact that it actually *did* happen. It is important to know what happened in the past, no matter how painful or fascinating, and to see how much we have grown as a country, continent, and world. You have the right and *privilege* of knowing the truth of your forefathers and how you have been shaped *because* of it. *Society* today is trying to erase the past and pretend it didn't happen or, worse yet, conceal the details from you, relinquish-

ing them from your mind. It is important to think about this fact and ask yourself why they would want to erase the knowledge of authentic past events from your mind. Think deeply about this question. How would you benefit from having yet another thing hidden from your mind? How many *political* things are currently hidden from you already? Are you willing to give up more of your privileged rights? Who or what is the source instigating this movement? Who benefits from attempting to erase historical facts from your information base? What does it solve by pretending historical events did not happen? What seems to be the reason for erasing historical facts from your mind? What is the end result of burying this disclosure? Does it change the fact that it really *did* happen? *Why* are they intent on doing this? Who appears to be funding the movement? What information can you gather to shed more light on this subject? Where can you find unbiased data so you can extrapolate and discover your own conclusion?

3. *Educational content.* Education at all levels should be, and was, a means for filling your mind with facts and actual events. The initial purpose was to grow in knowledge and gain a deeper understanding of how things work or operate, why things function the way they do, what actually happened, etc. The intent, and therefore the content, have changed from factual knowledge of your choosing to biased agendas of what *the system* wants you to believe. Why has society taken God out of schools? Who does this benefit? What appears to be the agenda for removing Him from the public school system? What about the information they are presenting in general? Is it based on fact, or is it biased? What might their agenda be? Who is behind curriculum changes in the educational system? Is there a common link? Why was there gradual and now progressive conformity in the chosen content? Who is funding them? What seems to be the reason for these changes? What appears to be the desired end result? What will this change? Are they over-

looking, ignoring, or leaving out information that doesn't support their agenda? Why might this be? Are they using unnecessary language or bias to sway the students' perception of *their* ideas or beliefs? What might their reasoning be for their efforts to influence you into accepting their biasing of what should be factual and educational information? Where can you find unbiased resources so you may assess this information? How will you determine which sources are reliable, credible, and fair? What do you think is going on? Evaluate the information you collect, and draw your own conclusion.

4. *Mandates.* Mandates are orders put in place by the authority of the one in a position to do so. What mandates are currently in effect in society today? Have you suddenly been *forced* to act, think, or respond in specific ways based on certain information presented to you? Who has provided this information? Who is funding it? What is the information on which the mandate is based upon? What seems to be the reason for the mandate? Has the information been presented in a way to *scare* you into doing something? Has there been action by intimidation? What appears to be the end or desired result of the mandate? Who does the mandate benefit? Does the source of the mandate appear to have an agenda? Is the source of the mandate overlooking, ignoring, or leaving out information that doesn't support the claims? Is any unnecessary information or language being used to sway your perception of the topic? Is there any censorship or *shaming* if you do not conform and agree? Does this mandate interfere with any of your freedoms? Where can you find unbiased research from an ethical and trusted source to help understand the mandate? How have others gained or profited from the mandate? How will you verify the credibility of the research and the source? Once verified, infer and draw your own conclusions based on the information you gathered. Follow the true and real science,

and extrapolate your own logical result. What have you discovered? Did you reach this decision without prejudice?

5. *Entertainment industry.* Entertainment used to be light-hearted and enlightening, with the supposed intention of providing a pleasurable experience and some needed relaxation. It was an opportunity to let your mind drift from your current world and slip into the make-believe events of someone or something else. Today a deliberate and intentional political message is portrayed and embedded in nearly all forms of entertainment, including movies, television shows, music, art, and even the advertising in between. Subliminal messages are most likely guaranteed to be a part of the included exposure. Are you familiar with all the subliminal messages encapsulated throughout all forms of entertainment?

Commercials and advertisements are all about propaganda. Their goal is to mesmerize and standardize *their* view and agenda and imprint it onto you, causing you to alter your reasoning and belief. What do you really know about subliminal messages? Where are subliminal messages hidden? What is their intent? Who benefits from them? How can you find out more about them? Why are people trying to influence you to *their* way of thinking and to *normalize* that, which is not normal, via commercials and entertainment content? In the entertainment realm, who is sending a political message? What seems to be the reason for this message? Does the message have a bias? What appears to be the desired end result? How could this affect you? To whom does this message benefit? Does the source of the entertainment appear to have an agenda? Are there any common links? Is the source ignoring, overlooking, or leaving out information that doesn't support its beliefs? Is the source using provocative, manipulative, or other biased language to sway the audience's perception? Maintain your own ability to think for yourself based on your own standards, and beware of any intent to influence you and your family. What information is being fed through all the electronic devices held so dearly? Who controls these devices? Are they secretly invasive in your home? What are these devices capable of? Where can you find unbiased and accurate information regarding all of this? What sources will you use in your research? How will you verify their credibility? What information is most relevant? Objectively analyze and evaluate this information and draw your own unprejudiced conclusion. What do you think is going on?

6. *Big Pharma and medicine.* Big Pharma has become a powerful entity of its own. You must do your own independent research to find out details about when, why, and whom they are. My goal is simply to bring awareness to this topic, not define the precise composition. A large conglomerate of drug sources and individual proprietors and then some comprise this entity of powerful control. There was a time when virtually the only source of drug advertising consisted of drug representatives propagating their product, attempting to influence physicians and other medical personnel with the intention of having their items chosen for a preferred drug formulary. Nowadays, not only is drug advertising in every venue, it now contains an inflamed sociopolitical agenda. In order to make a logical and informed decision regarding your choices and conclusions, ask yourself many fact-seeking questions.

Who is propagating the particular drug, vaccine, or other mechanism? Who is funding the propagation? Who is funding the clinical trials or research? What are they proposing? What seems to be the reason for doing this? What appears to be the desired end result? How could this change things? How can you verify safety and efficacy? Who would benefit from this product being chosen for use or consumption? Who would benefit from the sale of this product? How long has the product been on the market? How many years and what types of research were performed regarding the product? Did it go through all of the proper steps of research and studies? How will you verify this? Do they reveal what was used as a placebo—something "safety neutral," such as saline—or was it a previous version of a vaccine or other drug and thereby *not* neutral? Do they even use a placebo? Are the studies blinded? What is the premise of this product? Are there other products similar to it? What makes one better than the other? What other choices do you have? Does the source of the product appear to have an agenda? Is the source using unnecessary verbiage with the intent of swaying the perception of the consumer? How are medical staff being persuaded to utilize the product? Are there incentives for its usage? Are hospitals receiving *kickbacks* for certain drug use or even diagnoses? How can you find out this information? What reactions have occurred since the inception of the product? *Follow the money* and discover who receives monetary benefits in the medical domain. The ability to infer is vital in order to draw logical conclusions based on your findings. Where can you find untainted information? How will you verify your resources? What information is relevant for discovery in order to draw your own conclusions? Assess the information based on unbiased raw data and extrapolate potential outcomes. What do you think is going on?

7. *Social media.* Social media has taken the world by storm. Few, if any, cultures are not impacted by this form of communication. A choice can be made whether to use this device positively or negatively to affect, inform, or influence others. That is in the eye and decision of the beholder. Along with the favorable ability to connect with long-lost family, friends, or other people, social media has also become an unfavorable method of propagation and political influence. Who has devised the message? What seems to be the reason for the message? Is there a reason behind the timing of the message? What appears to be the desired end result of the message? How could this affect you? Who could be mainly affected? To whom does this

message benefit? Does the source of this message appear to have an agenda? Are there monetary rewards involved? Is the source of the message overlooking, ignoring, or leaving out pertinent information that doesn't support the beliefs or claim? Is there censorship to anyone with an opposing view? Does the source use particular verbiage or language to influence the reader or listener? Is there emotion built into the message? Is there an intent to instill fear in the viewer? Attempt to gather information from opposing viewpoints. Do not allow your own personal biases to cloud your judgment. How can you independently verify the information? Research the content and source. Collect as much raw data as possible. Use logic to evaluate the information. Identify evidence that forms your beliefs. Draw your own individual conclusion. What do you think is going on?

8. *Church and religion.* There is a distinct difference between your belief and a "religion." While a belief is a mental conviction of truth, and a church is a body of believers, a religion is a man-made title with rituals or *works* to be performed to gain approval. As mentioned previously, conduct your own research for detail and clarity. This section is meant to bring awareness to this particular topic. Propaganda and false prophets have been slipping into the church for centuries, and it continues today in even bigger and more obvious ways, although some ways are even more devious. This brings about the absolute need to evaluate information and engage in the process of critical thinking. Who is presenting the message? What seems to be the reason for the message? What is the desired end result of the message? Who is the message intended to glorify? How are you impacted by the message? In what ways are you affected? Who benefits from the message? Is there a financial incentive behind the message? Does the source of the message appear to have an agenda? Is there any political funding involved? Is the source overlooking, ignoring, or leaving out information that doesn't support its beliefs

or claims? Is the source using language meant to sway the parishioners' perception of the facts? What information is relevant to determine the answers? Where can you find unbiased information? Research this data from an unprejudiced perspective. Evaluate and analyze the information and ask yourself again, *who* is the focus of the *glory* of the message? Formulate your own conclusions. What has the information led you to discover?

9. *Politics.* Politics. Oh my, politics. What can be said about politics? In my belief, politics was intended to be *for the people.* The people were to elect officials who promised to work hard and *serve the people.* The *people* were supposed to be in control, not the government. It couldn't be further from this concept now. The political arena has become the center of self-serving agendas and a hub of propaganda. Thank goodness, this is not the case with every elected official. However, it is the majority. That being said, it is important to do your own research and decide for yourself the meaning and intention of political actions and agendas. Who is doing a specific action? What are they doing? What seems to be the reason for this action? Who is funding them? Why is it happening now? What are the intended end results of the action? How could this affect you? Who does this action benefit? Is there a monetary reward behind, or for, this action? Does the source of the action appear to have an agenda? Can you decipher what the agenda is? Is the source overlooking, ignoring, or leaving out information that doesn't support the beliefs or claims of the action? Is the source of the action using persuasive language to sway the people's perception of a fact? Is there censorship involved if there is an opposing view? Is there an intent to instill fear or intimidation in the people? Look at the opposing side of the source of action. Ask the same questions from an opposite perspective. Where do you find biases? What supports either view? How does this benefit either side? Independently research and verify the

information discovered. What sources will you use? How will you deem them reliable? What information is relevant for clarity? Evaluate the claims of opposing sides, keeping in mind potential biases. Allow yourself to see things from both perspectives. Draw a logical conclusion based on your findings. What did you discover? And always take advantage of your right and privilege to vote and make your opinion count.

10. *Legal system.* The legal system is tied completely to the political system, being a branch of it. Some officials of the court are elected, and some are not. The people elect some, and some are elected by the people we elected. Your own research will provide more clarity to these words. For the same reasons mentioned previously, it is important to ask the same questions regarding specifics in the legal system. Make yourself aware of potential bias and underlying reasons, such as financial, reputational, or even positional pressure. Always seek to find out who may be funding a person or event that may be occurring. Evaluate unbiased information you obtained through your own research. What do you conclude?

11. *Science and research.* Science *is* knowledge. It is a body of *facts* learned through study, observation, or experience. Generally, if you want to find the truth regarding something, material or organic, you follow the science. *However,* even science can be fabricated or manipulated by a human source. This again leads to the vital process of thinking critically. Regarding a new vaccine or a suspicious virus, rather than make assumptions or engage in a herd mentality, do your own research. Follow unbiased and true science. If someone or something is concealing evidence or will not reveal a source, it is important to ask yourself *why.* Who is making a scientific claim? What is the claim? What seems to be the reason for the claim? Are they offering full disclosure? What appears to be the end result of the claim? How could this affect you? How does this affect them? To

whom does this claim benefit? *Follow the money.* Are there monetary benefits for this claim? Are there monetary benefits based on a volume of people conceding to this claim? Does the source of the claim appear to have an agenda regarding it? Are there any other possible agendas involved? Is the source overlooking, ignoring, or leaving out information that doesn't support the claim? Is there censorship occurring for anyone with an opposing view? Is any unnecessary or persuasive language used to sway the end user's perception of the claim? Is there intimidation involved to promote the product? How about fear? Is there an intention meant to create fear in people? Where can you find information about sources that are not biased toward this claim? Research many unbiased sources as you seek answers and factual knowledge. Observe information from opposing sides of the claim. Is the research itself credible? Evaluate each side without prejudice. Determine the relevance of the information and focus on what is most important regarding the claim. Verify that the sources are credible. How will you determine if they are credible? Make sure you know who is funding the research you are examining. What would allow you to put something into your body without verifying facts regarding the ingredients? Know what goes into your body. Assess all of the information you gathered and analyze the data. Draw your own conclusion based on *your* research. Where does it take you? What conclusions do you arrive at?

12. *Literature.* Literature can be entertaining, informative, educational, persuasive, humorous, sad, etc. It can be almost anything. Writing has been a part of society for countless generations as a way of communicating, educating, and preserving thoughts and ideas. Unfortunately, literature can also be deceptive. Relating true, honest, accurate, and completely factual content is not required. So once again, it is important to ask many questions and consider the research you have personally collected regarding the liter-

ature and the source. Who is the author? What did they write? What seems to be the reason for writing the material? What appears to be the desired result of the material? How could this affect you? How could it affect the author? Who does it benefit? Does the author appear to have an agenda? Are you able to identify a political agenda? Is the author overlooking, ignoring, or leaving out information that may be contrary to the intended claim? Does the author use persuasive language to sway the readers' perception? Is there strong emotion or any emotion tied to the material? What can you learn about the opposing view if it poses an argument? How can you verify the facts or content within the material? Are they truthful? Is there some type of funding for the project? What unbiased sources can you use to find out more information? How will you verify the sources? Is the material meant for pleasure or to inform or persuade? Does the author reveal sources used for the material? Collect as much information as possible from credible sources. Evaluate the information objectively, and draw your own conclusion. What did you discover about the material? What about the author? What conclusion have you reached?

13. *Family, friends, or associates.* People you associate with can be very influential for numerous reasons. Perhaps you are fond of them, loyal, curious, indebted, opposed, or maybe even intimidated by them. Knowing the motive behind what people do, say, or even why can be challenging. It is important to be able to decipher the validity of the person and any motives or intentions they may have, especially regarding you. Sometimes there is controversy within your own family unit. Lately, it may even be derived from a politically different standpoint. Be able to identify the necessity to evaluate them as well. What are they doing, asking of you, or standing for? What seems to be the reason for this? What appears to be the desired end result? How would this affect you? How would it affect them?

Who does this action or request benefit? Do they appear to have an agenda? Are you able to identify the agenda? Is there political motivation? Are they overlooking, ignoring, or leaving out information contrary to their desire? Are they using persuasive or even deceptive language? Are they showing emotion in their request? Are they using manipulative tactics? Is there some way to challenge their view with an opposing viewpoint? What information can you draw from this? What questions can you ask them in order to gain more understanding of the situation? How can you become fully aware of the basis of the request? Ask yourself questions and critically think about the information you gathered. What conclusions have you reached based on the information?

This is just the tip of the iceberg. There are many additional ways in which your freedom is slipping away. Recall the massive iceberg that is said to have taken down the Titanic. The majority of this structure dwelled hidden in the depths of the same icy, dark waters it rested upon, yet was capable of enormous devastation against many odds. Just as the iceberg was deceiving, it is also possible for the information to be obscured or even deluded from the sphere of content made available to you while a multitude of hidden agendas lies beneath the surface...literally!

Take time to ask questions, perform research, and see the same things from a different perspective. Question the research, and challenge the validity of it. Know when it's time to pick your battles and dig a little deeper rather than take things at face value. You can't go wrong by discovering more.

> *The only freedom that is of enduring importance is the freedom of intelligence, that is to say, freedom of observation and of judgment, exercised on behalf of purposes that are intrinsically worthwhile. The commonest mistake made about freedom*

is, I think, to identify it with freedom of movement, or, with the external or physical side of activity.

—John Dewey

If you are influenced to think the way others think without first thinking for yourself, are you really free?

—Jill Fandrich

The most effective way to destroy people is to deny and obliterate their own understanding of their history.

—George Orwell

You can sway a thousand men by appealing to their prejudices quicker than you can convince one man by logic.

—Robert A. Heinlein

 Reflect:

1. Who is connecting your dots? If it is not you, who is it? Are you surprised by who or what is? What changes will you make as a result of the revelation?
2. Watch different news sources (with different owners), and listen to both sides of the same story. What is the basis for each opposing view?
3. Question the social media content and research facts about the topic at hand before formulating an opinion. Is there censoring involved? What have you discovered?
4. How can you gain more control over your thoughts and actions?
5. Define your moral code by which you evaluate incoming information. Use this basis to *ask questions* when presented with information.

6. How do you choose educational sources for yourself and your loved ones? Where do you research for the basis of the content? Do you know the academic content taught to other family members, especially children? How can you verify the intent of the content?
7. Identify and incorporate your core values into your mind's programming.
8. What do you do to protect yourself from conformity?
9. Identify the ways your freedom is being purloined. What other ways can you think of in which freedom is slipping away from you?

CHAPTER 2

What Is Critical Thinking?

What *is* critical thinking? It is the ability to observe and think about a situation and to see and assess the validity or reality of it based on your own research and analysis without outside influence or bias. *"Critical thinking is the analysis of an issue or situation and the facts, data or evidence related to it."*[1] You take time to see the essential truth based on logic and common sense. You challenge what has been said or shown and consider numerous possible answers or alternatives. The key is to ask questions wherever possible. Never stop asking questions. This is to be performed objectively without influence from personal feelings, opinions, or biases. The focus should be entirely based on factual information, perhaps even discovering new ways of thinking about things. You must be able to do this without being biased or prejudiced. Where is the evidence of proof? What is the source of evidence? Who is involved? Are they reliable? Is a source of funding somehow involved? How can you verify credibility? You have been blessed with tremendous brain power and the capacity to think critically. Use this ability to think with an open mind and consider the validity of the presented information.

Critical thinking is a skill that can be practiced and mastered. It allows you to make logical and informed decisions to the best of your abilities. There is no particular standard for how critical thinking occurs, and numerous approaches exist. However, some basic concepts that can guide you to become an exceptional critical thinker will be presented. It is important to *identify what is occurring*. What is the situation or problem at hand and the factors that may be influencing it? Gain clarity of the situation, including who and what may be influential. Ask questions such as *"Who is doing what?"* *"What seems to be the reason for this happening?"* and *"What are the end results, and how could they change?"*

The next step is to undergo intensive and independent *research*, comparing arguments about the issue of concern. Arguments are persuasive and influential. Therefore, it is important that your research is performed independently by you, and the resources must be verified as factual, reliable, credible, and unbiased. Evaluate the research and resources. Are the claims that are made "sourced" or "unsourced"? If the claims do not have a specified source, or you discover they are seeking to *hide* the source, that is a red flag, leading to the question of *why*. Continue to research this *new* question and add the data to the other collected information.

It is also important to be aware that the presented information may differ from what it *seems*. For example, a study may claim to use a placebo as a control. Yet, if you dig deeper, you may find it was not a *neutral* control, as in *all* vaccinations currently approved for the standard children's series of vaccinations presently given. None of them used a pure *neutral* placebo compared to the vaccine itself.[2]

Biases are sometimes very difficult to uncover, yet this is vital to the critical thinking process. The most skilled critical thinkers seek to master this difficult ability. Strong critical thinkers do their best to evaluate information objectively and view the claims of both sides of an argument. It is important to be able to wade through the waters of biases that likely are included on both sides. While *identifying biases*, it is equally important to set aside your own personal biases to ensure your judgment does not become clouded. Try challenging yourself to debate one side of the argument, justifying it until you win the argument. Then do *the same thing* for the opposing side of the argument! What have you learned from this exercise? Learn to see things from different vantage points and be objective in doing so. Analyze the evidence that forms your own beliefs, and verify that the sources are credible and reliable. Questions to ask when evaluating bias include,

"Whom does this benefit?" "Does the source of this information appear to have an agenda?" "Is the source overlooking, ignoring, or leaving out information that doesn't support its beliefs or claims?" and *"Is this source using unnecessary language to sway an audience's perception of a fact?"*

Next, it is important to use *logical reasoning* and draw conclusions based on the sound evidence you gathered. In order to master the skill of critical thinking, it is important to be able to *infer* and create an *educated* "guess" based on your thorough research. You must extrapolate and discover potential outcomes based on the raw data collected. Assess the information, and draw your own conclusion. As not all inferences will be correct, it becomes crucial to make a conscious effort to gather as much untainted information as possible before reaching this decision.

It can also be challenging yet important to *discern the relevance* of the information for your consideration and seek the most relevant data. There may be a multitude of data regarding the topic, and you must decipher what is most pertinent to reaching your desired direction. What is your end goal? Determine precisely what it is you desire to uncover or discover.

Finally, be open to *unbiased discovery* by asking open-ended questions. This allows all possibilities without prejudice. Unfiltered and unprompted information may be revealed by asking questions in this format. A free flow of information is encouraged, and there is a greater potential that productive information may be produced that may further guide your evaluation of data.

Research and find additional ways to perform the skill of critical thinking. While there are many methods to implore this process, we discussed the need to *identify what is occurring, research, identify biases,* use *logical reasoning, discern the relevance* of the information, and partake in an *unbiased discovery* by asking open-ended questions. Develop your own process of critical thinking, and begin to utilize it in all scenarios throughout your day. You will find that if you practice it enough, it will become second nature, and you will be able to better formulate unbiased conclusions by utilizing this process.

As an example of a scenario to think critically about, I was driving up the street on my way home, and I approached a red traffic light. I then came to a stop behind a sporty new Corvette. After admiring the car, I looked to my right and noticed a healthy-looking young woman bound by a mask in a car by herself. I began to critically think immediately. The identified issue was wearing a mask in a car by yourself. As a medical professional, I understand viruses are so tiny in comparison to the woven binding of face masks. I asked myself the first critical thinking question, "If viruses are too small to be stopped by a mask, how could it be logical to wear a mask with the intention of preventing the inhalation of any type of virus?" I based this first question on substantiated research I already knew. Who does this benefit? What could cause someone to do this? How could it prevent the exhalation from penetrating the surface based on the same logic? What other effects may it have? I continued using common sense as I thought critically. How could she be at risk if she sat alone and in her own space? What is the most relevant information to substantiate this act? Isn't the body designed with the ability to fight off foreign objects, such as bacteria and viruses? As a matter of fact, isn't the body's defense mechanism the *best* method of fighting them off? What would eventually be the effect on the body of blocking natural airflow into the lungs for an extended period of time? What would the inhaled mask fibers do to the body through time? What are the masks made of? My answer became obvious to me by using logical reasoning. I found no benefit to wearing a mask for a virus, especially in an environment of my own, by myself. And it can be substantiated by performing research through trusted sources, *with no agenda,* that give honest answers. What would cause this woman to be so fearful that she is wearing a basic mask, which is ineffective for viruses, and afraid to breathe fresh air openly while riding solo in a confined vehicle? *Fear* has been known to stand for *false events appearing real.* So why is she living in fear? Who instilled this fear in her? What is the source of the fear? What seems to be the reasoning for this fear? What appears to be the desired results of instilling fear in someone? Who does this benefit? Do *they* have an agenda? Has the source of the fear overlooked, ignored, or left out information that doesn't support its agenda? Is the source using unnecessary language to cause fear? Is there a financial incentive for *the source?* An entirely new round of critical thinking questions has evolved from the situation.

What causes people to blindly fall into a herd mentality without questioning the details behind it all? One method, as old as time yet obviously still effective, is intimidation by *fear*. If you scare people enough, you will be able to exert control over them, even to the point that they hide their faces while alone and seclude themselves from public interaction. That is a very severe depiction yet a very real example of what the world has just experienced. Back in 2018 or 2019, would you ever have imagined willingly choosing to abandon all outside activity, including your commute to work, and *hiding* indoors from something that cannot even be seen? When you instill enough fear into people, they become willing to abandon critical thought and fall prey to the control of the ones leading the charge. How did the media participate in this event? Who funded the media? Is the media guilty of *outrage*? Observe all of the volatile words they use to gain control over you and your emotions in an attempt to influence and control you. Words such as *outrage, corruption, attacks,* and *urgent,* and phrases like *witch hunt, last chance, breaking news,* etc., are all designed to appeal to your emotions and cause you to *submit* to their authority. They are meant to spark fear in order to cease your ability to critically think and use logic. Do you want to be constantly *riled up* by words such as these? How would your health be affected if you were constantly being inflamed? Why do they feel they must strike you with emotional words in order to win your attention? *If the source believed in its own cause, there wouldn't be a need to use manipulation.* Do you feel the media's agenda is more important to them than *you* are as a person deserving of the truth and the ability to think for yourself and make your own sound decisions based on facts?

Ways to avoid getting caught up in the hysteria

1. *Become mindfully aware.* It all begins with awareness. Take a step back, or maybe two, and assess the situation. Be mindful of the source of information. Who is causing the hysteria? What seems to be the reason for this happening?

What seems to be the desired end result of the hysteria? How could this change things? Whom does this hysteria benefit? Does the source of this information appear to have an agenda? What is their agenda? Who is funding the source? Is the source overlooking, ignoring, or leaving out information that doesn't support its beliefs or claims? Is the source censoring people if they present with differing viewpoints? Is the source using persuasive or intimidating language to sway your perception? Are they relying on their ability to ignite your emotions in order for them to hook your attention and reel you into their side? Are they just trying to share unbiased and informative facts, or are they emotionally charged in their approach? What does it appear their goal is for you? To arouse your emotions? Ask yourself questions about the situation, and make yourself aware of as much information as possible. Be open to all angles and possibilities. You may still agree to side with them after critically thinking, but at least allow yourself the opportunity to consider the occurrence from an unbiased perspective, asking questions in the process. Be aware of how they have chosen to engage with you.

2. *Meditate.* Take time to regain control of your senses and emotions. Now that you are aware of what they are attempting to do, take some deep breaths and find a way to relax. There are many effective methods of meditation to choose from. Find a quiet and serene room to calm yourself and bring yourself to a peaceful high-frequency vibration. Clear your thoughts of all biases and prejudices, and come to a place of honest contentment. Let your mind rest, and let your positive energy expand. Practice and explore various forms of meditation until you find the one that works best for you.

3. *Pray.* Just as you are able to clear your mind with meditation, you may clear your mind by focusing on your Creator and praising Him for all of your blessings. Place your trust in Him and in the name of Jesus Christ. *"Let go, and let*

God," as the saying goes. Be thankful for all that you have and are able to do. Praise and gratitude are two powerful qualities that can bring you to a place of tranquility in His precious name. Thank God for your freedom and ability to critically think without bias. Conversationally talk to God, and know He is with you at all times and through every event you encounter. Lean on Him, and nail your fears and concerns to the cross of Jesus Christ. Allow the peace beyond all understanding to flow through every cell of your body. Pray for discernment as you wade through the ever-changing waters you encounter each day. There are many wonderful prayers that can be found online on every topic imaginable. Discover what prayers flow the best for you, or create your own. Let the Holy Spirit be your guide.

4. *Critically think.* Ask yourself questions regarding the situation, as discussed previously in this chapter. Who is doing what? What seems to be the reason for the situation happening? What are the desired end results for this happening? How could this change things? Who does this benefit? Does the source of this information appear to have an agenda? What is the underlying agenda? Is the source overlooking, ignoring, or leaving out information that does not support its beliefs or claims? Is the source using unnecessary persuasive language in order to sway an audience's perception of the fact? Is it healthy for you to run with an *outraged* point of view? Does it benefit your family? Is it beneficial to your business or career? What might the consequences be if you submit to the intimidation of hysteria? What purpose would this serve? Do they care for your well-being? What causes people to use intimidation as a method of influence? Is it an ethical way to try to get your way? Is it professional? Are there any other ways to interpret the message? What are the details of the opposing view? Perform extensive research on this and any other additional unbiased questions that come to mind. Analyze this information, verifying that the sources are valid and credible.

Determine the relevance of the collected information, and draw your own conclusion based on the unbiased, raw data.

5. *Stop the flow of information.* Turn the television off. Close the news app, Internet, or YouTube coverage. Is there another source of information you can choose that is unbiased? Perhaps you could back away from the information altogether? This is what I chose to do, and I went from being highly sensitized to being calm, relaxed, and peaceful, and I am engaging in a much more pleasurable way of life. Whenever I peek back in to see the "temperature" of the news sources, nothing has ever changed. Challenge yourself to shut off the valve of all news sources for a week. Assess the condition of your mind after this week. Assess your emotions. Do you notice any difference? Perhaps try for two weeks. Monitor, or even journal, regarding the results.

6. *Believe.* What is your belief system? Who do you believe in? Is this method aligned with your belief system? Do you feel a sense of tranquility at the thought of pursuing the message? Your beliefs should lead you to a trusting place of serenity. Does this lead you there? Focus on your beliefs, and let that direct your choices. Focus on what is good and what you know to be right and true. Do not let others intimidate you or influence you under false pretenses. Know your core values, and let this be your guide. Define them, and align with them. Put any questions you have through the critical thinking process.

7. *Distract.* What is important to you? Is it more important to focus on your family and their needs? How about a hobby you enjoy? Is there a venue you could serve in to help others? There are many activities you could engage in that are more productive than allowing the hysteria to consume you. Pour your heart and soul into your business, church, or community service. Evaluate your priorities and disengage from the emotionally harmful noise. Where can you

be a blessing to others? Who can you positively impact? How can you leave an enlightened footprint in this world?

Misery loves company, and a potential goal of the news outlets is to combine and *conform* as many people as possible as there is power in numbers. Once you add the factor of fear, you now have *control* as well. In that same mindset, isn't it time to band together (yet as individuals) with like-minded people in your own crusade, aligned with your values and for the right reasons, to protect your own freedoms? It is time to take action. Too much time has been spent in blind ignorance, closing eyes to the rapidly changing and progressing movement, to erase history and live by fear and discontentedness, always looking for a reason to be highly sensitized. It's time to become fully aware of what your children and the younger generation, in general, now must face and the battle for their very souls.

Critical thinking requires constantly updating your knowledge as you take in new information. You must look at your own biases and be logical in your reasoning. Look at things for yourself. Make your own decisions, and be able to see more than one side of every issue. Take the emotion away, and think of the facts at hand. Carefully listen to the input of others and consider, yet know yourself enough to be able to make *your own* independent, informed, and logical decision. Be open-minded while using truth-seeking reasoning. There is an art to being able to disconfirm the claims of others but done in such a way as to promote a common bond or shared fate. This would result in an *intensely* more powerful influence than intimidation or deceit. Use your mind without prejudice and fear, and learn to see things from opposing vantage points. Evaluate information from different perspectives, be open-minded for consideration, yet stand firm in your final, unprejudiced conclusion. Think for yourself, and *never* stop asking questions.

> *Responsibility to yourself means refusing to let others do your thinking, talking, and naming for you; it means learning to respect and use your own*

brains and instincts; hence, grappling with hard work.

> —Adrienne Rich

The important thing is not to stop questioning. Curiosity has its own reason for existing.

> —Albert Einstein

When we blindly adopt a religion, a political system, a literary dogma, we become automations. We cease to grow.

> —Anaïs Nin

Critical thinking requires us to use our imagination, seeing things from perspectives other than our own and envisioning the likely consequences of our position.

> —Bell Hooks

Nothing is more conducive to peace of mind than not having any opinions at all.

> —Georg Christoph Lichtenberg

Whenever we hear an opinion and believe it, we make an agreement, and it becomes part of our belief system.

> —Miguel Ruiz

People can be extremely intelligent, have taken a critical thinking course, and know logic inside and out. Yet they may just be clever debaters, not critical thinkers, because they are unwilling to look at their own biases.

> —Carol Wade

Reflect:

1. What is critical thinking? What is the process of critical thinking?
2. Think about a topic that strikes an emotion. Now engage in critical thinking, and ask yourself the series of critical thinking questions regarding that topic with an open mind and without prejudice.
3. What are the ways mentioned to avoid getting caught up in hysteria? What else can you add to this list?
4. How can you become more aware of potential environmental manipulation? Can you remove your own bias and listen open-mindedly, considering opposing vantage points?
5. How do you use distractions to *break away* from emotionally charged information?
6. Find a meditation of choice and perform. Learn to transform your energy into positive, uplifting vibrations.
7. Practice asking critical-thinking questions in selected situations throughout each day.

CHAPTER 3

Where Does Your Obedience Lie?

*Control the manner in which a man interprets his world, and
you have gone a long way toward controlling his behavior.*
—Stanley Milgram

In 1961, psychologist Stanley Milgram began preparation for a series
of social psychology experiments, known as the Milgram experiments, measuring the willingness of men to obey an authority figure
who *"instructed them to perform acts conflicting with their personal
conscience."*[3] The basis of these experiments was obedience to authority figures. The experiments began a year after the trial of Adolf
Eichmann in Jerusalem with the intent of answering the question,
*"Could it be that Eichmann and his million accomplices in the Holocaust
were just following orders? Could we call them all accomplices?"*
(Milgram 1974). Milgram was examining justifications for acts of
genocide offered by those accused at the World War II Nuremberg
war criminal trials. The defense they used was based on the excuse of
obedience. They claimed they were "just following orders" from their
superiors.

Participants in this experiment were led to believe they were
assisting an unrelated experiment in which they had to administer electric shocks, ranging from a mild initial shock of 15 V and
extending to a severe and dangerous 450 V shock to a person in
another room who was a student learning. The shocks were given

upon each incorrect answer the student provided, with each one progressively more intense. In reality, this other person was an actor. Yet the participant was led to believe that for each wrong answer, the student would receive an electrical shock at variably increasing volts, including a level considered fatal. In reality, there was no such punishment actually occurring. Prerecorded blood-curdling sounds were prepared to add to the ambience of shock therapy.

It was found that a large percentage of participants would fully obey the instructions despite being uncomfortable. When the participant refused to administer a shock, the experimenter was to give a series of four orders to encourage and ensure that they continued. They displayed varying degrees of tension and stress as a result, including sweating, trembling, stuttering, biting their lips, groaning, nervous laughing fits, seizures, and digging their fingernails. Every participant paused the experiment at least once to question it. After being assured by the experimenter, all participants continued on with the experiment to 300 V, and two-thirds continued to the full 450 V, which is a potentially fatal level.

Milgram summarized the experiment in his 1974 article "The Perils of Obedience," writing, "*The legal and philosophic aspects of obedience are of enormous importance, but they say very little about how most people behave in concrete situations. I set up a simple experiment at Yale University to test how much pain an ordinary citizen would inflict on another person simply because he was ordered to by an experimental scientist. Stark authority was pitted against the subjects' strongest moral imperatives against hurting others, and, with the subjects' ears ringing with the screams of the victims, authority won more often than not. The extreme willingness of adults to go to almost any lengths on the command of an authority constitutes the chief finding of the study and the fact most urgently demanding explanation. Ordinary people, simply doing their jobs, and without any particular hostility on their part, can become agents in a terrible destructive process. Moreover, even when the destructive effects of their work become patently clear, and they are asked to carry out actions incompatible with fundamental standards of morality, relatively few people have the resources needed to resist authority.*"

Milgram was interested in discovering how far people would go regarding obeying an instruction, even at the cost of harming another person. There came a point where the participants no longer saw themselves as responsible for their actions and proceeded to evoke what they thought was harm onto another person. They became *a vessel* to carry out the instructions of another and submit to their authority, regardless of the consequence. Online research will lead you to many summaries of this experiment and related links for more information. Take some time to learn more about these experiments and the interpretations that resulted.

How do you see this happening in the world today? Can you see any examples in your life that replicate or are a variation of these types of actions? Could it be that people will just blindly follow authority, even at the risk of harming another person? What people in authority today have the opportunity to do this very same action? Have you ever been in this position, either as the one in authority or as the participant? How can you use critical thinking skills to reason out a logical answer to this dilemma?

Thoughts about the Milgram experiment

1. *Personalization.* The students were not personalized to the participants. There is a lot to be said about human nature and personal relationships. When you know someone intimately, the close bond creates an emotional attachment, making it more difficult to consider any sense of harm. Whereas in the experiments, not knowing the students personally allowed the participants to disconnect from the emotional aspect of the experiment, excluding the morality-conscience variable that was present. This variable was able to be overcome in the name of science and also via submission to the authority of the experimenter in charge. Do you think the results would have been different if a personal relationship existed between the participants and the students or, in this case, the actors? How would you have responded if you were a participant and you person-

31

ally knew the student? What if the student was a family member or other loved one? What if you didn't know the student? What if *you* were the student? Would your relationship with the student bear any relevance on the decision you would make to or not to inflict harm on someone stemming from orders from an authority figure? How about for a cause? How else might *you* be affected in your obedience to authority regarding issues of relationships with another? As the world becomes smaller and your freedoms continue to slip away, consider how you may be placed in a situation of obedience versus relationships. How would you respond if a similar occurrence happened in your work, group, social, or organizational settings? Consider how you would handle this situation. What other critical-thinking questions would you ask regarding the relationship factor?

2. *Obedience for a cause.* Most of the participants, even if reluctant, continued to inflict what they believed to be painful electric shocks upon students because that is what they were told to do. At one point or another, each one requested confirmation for assurance that they were doing the right thing and received it. Some were said to have proceeded in the name of science, believing they were responding to what they considered to be a *good cause.* How would you react in this scenario? If presented with the same situation, would you blindly follow orders because you were told to do so, knowing you were severely hurting a random person? Or would you blindly follow orders in the name of science or for some other good cause? Would you critically think about whether or not it would be okay to inflict harm upon another innocent person for any reason? Would you obey like a loyal dog given an order? Or would your innate sense of morality prevent you from inflicting pain? Think of a scenario in your environment today where a cause of importance to you comes to mind. What are you willing to do for this cause? Would you allow harm to be inflicted upon someone else, whether the person is known person-

ally or not, for the sake of the cause? Who would benefit from this occurring? Would you have a moral dilemma if the reason was for a cause? What factors would make this okay in your mind? What factors would cause it to be not okay? How would you be affected if you were put in this situation? What if *you* were the one afflicted? How would you feel on the opposing side of the situation? Would your values come into play? How will you prepare for a similar situation to potentially affect you today? What other critical thoughts come to mind?

3. *Herd mentality.* It has been said and is proven to be true, that there is strength in numbers. As the participants observed their peers continuing to shock students despite the blood-curdling pain responses, they claimed they felt more justified as they were following suit. In society today, do you see evidence of this type of behavior? When more and more people come together, is there a growing strength and conviction in their actions and inhibitions? Have you ever found yourself in a situation where you had a certain belief, but because of the crowd or group you were entangled with, you changed your choice and followed the crowd? What were the circumstances? How have you been influenced when the majority of people made it clear your choice or opinion was *wrong*, and theirs was *right*? Did you stand your ground for what you believed in? It is difficult to go against the grain. Think about how determined salmon are to swim against the current to migrate back to their origins. They are not influenced by the current flowing in the opposite direction or any other neighboring creatures among them. Nothing can prevent them from doing what they know they must do. What questions come to mind about how you react to differing crowds? What would happen if you stood your ground? Would you be willing to harm another person based on the influence of a crowd or group? Have you considered what their intentions are or what they are saying or thinking? Is there a happy medium

between your viewpoint and theirs? Or deep down, do you still believe your original thought? How can you assess the situation and verify that you align with your values? Your values are being challenged by an increasing rate (of alarm) daily. Identify your own moral code and belief system, and align your thoughts and actions with your values. What must you do to intensify your convictions so you are less likely to sway from them? How can you remain firm in your own decisions based on your individual values? What other critical questions can you ask to further explore this common scenario?

4. *Intimidation.* There is a right and a wrong expression of authority. Recall your own innate sense of right and wrong, your code of morality. Your conscience will guide you if something is not right. It is important to have order in society and to be obedient to the laws of the land. But how would you respond under intimidating circumstances? In the experiment, the participants were reassured that they were to follow the experimenter. He was in authority, which is indirectly an element of intimidation. What may result if the rules aren't followed? Would there be a penalty? Would they become *the student* and be subjected to shocks? What part of intimidation is responsible for how someone reacts? In a similar scenario, how would you be affected by intimidation? Would you react a certain way in anticipation of a negative result if you did not comply? What would happen if you obeyed, knowing there was an infliction of pain upon another person? What would happen to you if you disobeyed? Would you have a mental dilemma regarding your choices? How would the program be affected if you didn't obey? In society, are you strong enough to choose what you consider to be right despite an intimidating outcome? How about despite intimidating pressure? What forms of intimidation reach and affect you? How do you respond to them? How can you overcome them? Think of a scenario today where you are being pressured

in an intimidating manner. What are the circumstances? What are your options in how to respond? Will your values be compromised? What are your values? Are they clearly defined? Are you willing to fight for them? Are you secure with who you are, and are you willing to stand up for your values despite intimidation? How will you know what to stand up for if your core values are not defined? Prepare for how you would respond to intimidation in your current environment.

5. *Code of ethics.* Are you good with your word? Perhaps some of the participants continued because they committed themselves to the experiment. There was an ethical obligation to participate because they said they would. Do *you* do what you say and say what you do? What do you stand for? *Whom* do you stand for? What can you think of that would cause you to back out of what you said you would do? Where do you draw the line? What is your own personal ethics code? How would you respond if you committed to something, then realized later it violated your values somehow? What effects would this have on you? Where does your loyalty lie? How do your values affect the choices you make? Do you discover what a project or commitment entails before agreeing to pursue it? How can you prevent this situation from happening in the first place? What questions can you ask before you give your word or sign on the dotted line? Will you allow your values to be compromised?

6. *Location.* The setting may have been an influential factor in the experiment. Perhaps the industrial-like or professional lab-type setting affected the participants. How would a formal location affect people? How might a softer setting make any difference? How would the technical equipment affect the participants? What effect would the sight and thought of the shock machine have on them? How about the proximity to the students? How are you affected by location? Do you respond differently in a "sterile" environ-

ment as compared to a cozy, friendly environment? Would your values be defended differently in either case? What type of location would affect your decisions? Think about how you would respond to authority in your workplace versus a family setting. Would you compromise your values in either one?

7. *Demeanor of the experimenter.* Perhaps the personality and demeanor of the one in charge swayed the degree of obedience. What effect could a certain personality have on the participants? What if the experimenter was gentle? What if the experimenter was brash and unapproachable? Would the personality have any effect at all? How do you handle situations when the one in authority has a distinct personality? How do you respond to a gentle persuasion? How about a brazen persuasion? What would you do differently in each situation? What if you discover the authority figure has a mentally challenged personality, such as narcissism? How would you respond, knowing there is an embedded lack of concern or compassion for others? How is your performance affected by a shy leader? How about an aggressive leader? Have you ever let your values become compromised based on personality? How can you prepare yourself to do the *right* thing in your eyes, no matter what personality you are dealing with?

8. *Settings.* Along with the location, perhaps the colors in the room affected the processing of information. Could the layout of the room and the chosen decor have affected the "personality" of the room? How could the temperature affect the participants? Was the temperature warm, cool, or comfortable? What other sounds could be heard? Were there any defining scents or odors that could have affected the participants? How would the sound of the blood-curdling screams affect them? How does a setting affect how you respond to authority? Would different settings change your responses in any way? How does temperature affect you? What if there were extreme temperatures? Would you

be persuaded? How does lighting, colors, or smells affect your decision-making process? Would any of it affect your obedience to authority? Would compassion prevail over obedience? Or would obedience stand as the decision made to honor authority despite setting variations? Is there a factor regarding the degree of the screams or moans? Would the intensity cause differing responses? What other factors could be influential to you? How can you prepare yourself to stand firm in your own values without prejudice or influence?

How far are you willing to go for the sake of obedience? Where does your obedience lie? Or maybe, *how* does your obedience *lie*? Do you clearly delineate what is acceptable and what borders on wrong or immoral? For the most part, it is important to be obedient to authority. However, when something occurs against your moral code, or you have this uneasy feeling or sense that something just isn't right, ask questions. Critically think about all aspects of the situation at hand, and find out as much information as possible. Consider both sides of the story, and weigh the possibilities. Do not blindly follow the crowd if you do not know where they are going or if you know something isn't as it should be. Be authentic. Stand by your innate sense of right and wrong, and critically think your way to a resolution you can live with. Be brave and endure the process, guided wisely by *your* defined values.

> *The disappearance of a sense of responsibility is the most far-reaching consequence of submission to authority.*
> —Stanley Milgram

> *It may be that we are puppets—puppets controlled by the strings of society. But at least we are puppets with perception, with awareness. And perhaps our awareness is the first step to our liberation.*
> —Stanley Milgram

It is not so much the kind of person a man is as the kind of situation in which he finds himself that determines how he will act.

—Stanley Milgram

The essence in obedience consists in the fact that a person comes to view himself as an instrument for carrying out another person's wishes and he therefore no longer regards himself as responsible for his actions.

—Stanley Milgram

Each individual possesses a conscience which to a greater or lesser degree serves to restrain the unimpeded flow of impulses destructive to others. But when he merges his person into an organizational structure, a new creature replaces autonomous man, unhindered by the limitations of individual morality, freed of humane inhibition, mindful only of the sanctions of authority.

—Stanley Milgram

 Reflect:

1. What was the objective of the Milgram experiments?
2. Read three different versions of the experiments and the summaries they provide.
3. How do you respond to authority when it is aligned with your values?
4. How do you respond to authority when it is *not* aligned with your values?
5. Think about a controversial issue regarding obedience. Ask yourself three unbiased questions from the point of view that you favor. Next, ask yourself three unbiased questions from the opposing point of view and consider all responses objectively and with an open mind.

6. How would you respond if you were in a group, and nine people thought one way, and you thought another? Would you alter your view or stand your ground? What if they put pressure on you? What if only *you* put pressure on you because you thought differently? What critical thinking questions could you ask to assess the situation properly?

7. In a situation regarding obedience, how would you respond to volatile words like *outrage, shocking, urgent*, etc.? Would you be intimidated to respond if someone was pressuring you? Ask yourself five critical-thinking questions the next time you feel someone is trying to manipulate you by intimidation.

8. How can you stand by your innate sense of right and wrong and remain obedient? Is this even possible?

CHAPTER 4

How Do You Decide?

You are intelligent and able to process large amounts of information. You have a tremendous ability to think and consider multiple and even complex situations and potential responses. This separates you from other creatures, and each person has the opportunity to be authentic and to think for him or herself. So how do you take advantage of this opportunity? What is your primary mode of decision-making? Do you have a hunger or drive for something? Or maybe it is based on a need or outside influence? Why might you be affected by the influence of others? Let's examine possible methods.

Methods of decision-making

1. *Critical thinking.* This is the desired method of decision-making. As mentioned earlier, critical thinking is a multifaceted method of asking unbiased questions from different angles of a situation. After you have clearly identified the situation or issue, gather facts and relevant information in an untainted manner and consider more than one vantage point. Without prejudice, seek to discover and collect content before formulating an educated inference. Be sure to gather as much information as possible and to ascertain the credibility of the sources you used for research and the relevance of the contents. Understand reasons why

you are drawn to one viewpoint versus another. Is there an influential reason? With critical thinking, you want to be a *blank slate* as you gather the data. Yet as you have thoroughly processed all potential avenues, bring forth your innate sense of right and wrong as a guide, along with your carefully chosen objective evidence in drawing a conclusion. Allow logic and common sense to be your GPS, and navigate to a decision that is emotion-free in its origins.

2. *Intimidation.* Unfortunately, there are many things in life that become, or perhaps always have been, intimidating. As you progress through different stages of life, the object of intimidation may change, yet likely, there will be intimidating factors lurking. What comes to mind as an intimidating factor in your life? Or possibly, who? When you hear the word intimidation, what instinctively comes to mind? Is it a person, a financial event, a location, a status, or maybe a situational event? How do you handle intimidation? Do you give in to the influence and allow your values to be compromised? Or do you proceed with your own agenda despite it? Are some situations more intimidating than others? How do they affect you? Do you allow intimidation to control how you make decisions? How can you build up a tolerance against intimidation? How can you avoid intimidating people or circumstances? Prepare yourself to remain strong and convicted in your values, notwithstanding any attempts from others of intimidation. If possible, attempt to view things from both perspectives and consider all possibilities. Analyze all information you gathered through trusted sources, and draw your own conclusions from the data at hand. Ultimately, critically think through intimidating factors, and do not allow them to compromise your values.

3. *Reputation.* Are you influenced by how people perceive you? This is very common in younger generations, as proven by social media, yet it can be influential to young and old alike. It is human nature to want to be accepted

by others. But is this a powerful factor in your life that you will allow to be the determining factor in making decisions? In particular, what if a morality issue was on the line? Would you base your decision on the issue by observing your conscience, or would you base it on how you will *look best* on social media? How much time do you spend on social media? Do you focus on the number of followers you have or how many people respond to "like" something you have posted? What causes the opinions of social media participants to value this digital form of acceptance more than in-person comradery? Do you partake for fun with no influential concern for responses, or do you rely on interactions for a form of popularity or acceptance? How about in a work setting? Do you make decisions a certain way due to your reputation? What about other settings, such as social, community, or family situations? Does your reputation in any setting affect how you make decisions? Do you or are you willing to compromise your values for your reputation?

4. *Herd mentality.* There truly is power in numbers, and inhibitions can be altered as well. For whatever reason, some people feel *safe* within a group and may be inclined to *become* what they are all about. A good example of this is found in gangs. The premise of a gang is to find security in a group of people and feel accepted. In the process, the group generally thinks as one unit, groupthink, in the hopes and expectations of acceptance. Often, they may not even be *permitted* to think for themselves. They lost their individuality and gave in to conformity. Possibly, at this point, there may even be a *penalty* if they attempt to leave the group. There are many other groups of like-minded people as well. In a group, it is important to have the freedom and safety to still be able to think and speak for yourself. Are you permitted to be authentic? Do you follow in line with the majority? Who benefits from being in the group? Who controls the group? What are your reasons for being within the group? Do you consider all informa-

tion and then formulate your own opinion? How do you respond if the majority is in an agreement that violates your morals? If you respond with an opposing view, how do they react to you? Would you still be accepted? Or would you be in danger? Is the group mellow or volatile? What seems to be the agenda of the group? Are you strong enough to stand up for your own beliefs and make your own independent decisions?

5. *Peer pressure.* Peer pressure is not just a concern in the school system for teenage-range people. It also exists within every age group and in every realm. The premise of peer pressure, like herd mentality, is to be accepted by others. Sometimes you may be challenged to do something or act in a certain way based on the promptings of someone else. Perhaps it is a coworker or even a boss. It could stem from a group of friends or even family. Whatever the source, how are you affected by pressure from peers? Who is applying the pressure? What seems to be the desired goal of the pressure? How does the pressure affect your ability to make decisions? Do you allow them to influence you and sway your decisions? Do you consider the validity of their request or insistence? Identify the situation, and allow yourself to listen to their side of the issue. Consider the source, and if more information is needed to substantiate the claim, proceed in performing your own individual research. Find out as many facts regarding the situation as possible. Evaluate all of the data. Next, align the information with your values. What are potential options to resolve the situation? Independently draw your own conclusions. Did you come to the same conclusions as they did, using an unbiased critical-thinking method? If your conclusion differs, are you confident enough to stand firm in your decision, which aligns with your values? What types of pressures from other people affect you? What are some ways you can avoid peer pressure in the first place? How can you create an environ-

ment where peer pressure is minimized, if not eliminated, altogether?

6. *Financial advantage.* Financial incentives are intriguing and most likely appealing. But what is the premise of the incentive? Is it in exchange for a worthy service, object, or event? Or is there a persuasive nature, requesting you to sway to a certain side of an issue? How might you be influenced by a financial persuasion, even if it is set against your sense of what is right? Or can you choose the *right* option despite a prosperous reward for choosing the *wrong* side? Is there a dollar amount that is a deciding factor? Are there any other extenuating circumstances that would tag on to a decision based on a financial advantage? How would you handle a significantly prosperous request that clashed with your morals? How can you guard yourself against allowing a financial incentive to sway your decisions when your values are concerned?

7. *Fear.* Fear encompasses numerous possibilities, each different for every individual. What are some of your fears? What is your biggest fear? Do you have a fear of abandonment or of being alone? Do you have a fear of missing out on something (FoMo) or maybe a general fear, such as a fear of the unknown? There may be a fear derived from not being accepted or perhaps a fear of harm if you don't conform to a certain way or opinion. Identify your greatest fear. How would this fear shape the way you make decisions if it came into play? Would it cause you to make a decision differently than if the fear was not present? Would it cause you to make a decision against your morals or belief system? Would any of your values be compromised? How can you *reframe* this fear and see it in a new light? Is there any conditioning you can perform or things to avoid, to desensitize, or even remove yourself from the fear? Identify ways to separate this fear from your decision-making opportunities.

8. *Emotionally charged.* An emotionally charged person, especially a group, could have a distinct impact on a situation.

People that are emotionally charged often respond *based* on emotions rather than logic. It is difficult not to be affected by this type of volatile demeanor, especially if you are a well-controlled person. The negative vibrations are infectious and spread rapidly. Many movements today are actually *based* on emotions themselves rather than logic. How do you respond when you are with someone running on high emotions? Are you influenced to side with them just to keep the peace? Or maybe out of fear? How do you respond when you are within a group that becomes highly charged? Would you have a tendency to conform to the intense energy? Are you still able to hold true to your beliefs? How would you handle the emotional intensity if it was in contrast to your values? Identify ways you could remove yourself from the emotion in this type of situation, and allow yourself to critically think your way to an unbiased resolution.

9. *Spiritually charged.* Sometimes there is a spiritual realm that may draw people to a decision. It may not necessarily be based on what is right versus wrong but rather it is *spiritually* driven. This method may build on passion or a desire, also with an emotional attachment. How would you handle something of this persuasion? Do you still respond based on your core values? Perhaps it's a matter of *how* you react that is of concern. Have you ever been overly passionate about a cause you believed in and responded in a way you normally wouldn't have? Do you let passion alter the way you respond? How might you respond if your beliefs were being jeopardized? Are you able to look at both sides indiscriminately? What information can you gather that might be helpful in reaching a logical conclusion? How can you hold your own emotions at bay while taking an unbiased look at both sides? How can you avoid potential situations that contradict your values in the first place? Collect as much information as possible without prejudice,

then draw a logical solution rather than "drinking the Kool-Aid."

10. *Loyalty.* Loyalty is an admirable character quality to possess *if* it is aligned with your values. What or who are you loyal to? What are the reasons for the loyalty? To what extent will you devote your allegiance? What would you do if the object of your loyalty was compromised? How would you respond if you were challenged regarding your loyalty? Would your loyalty trump over values? What is the opposing perspective on the situation? Is there a reasonable premise? Will this cause you to alter how you respond? How far would you take loyalty when it coincides with your values? How far would you take it if it *contradicts* your values? If trust was broken, how would you handle the situation? Will your loyalty ever cause you to compromise your values? How does loyalty affect how you make decisions?

11. *Obedience.* Stanley Milgram based his experiments on the effects of human nature on obedience. How do you relate to the participants in Milgram's experiments? Would obedience to an authority figure affect your decision to do something against your values? What about obedience to someone you trust and love? Could that possibly lead you to compromise your values? Is there a scenario that would cause you to alter your belief system in the name of obedience? Are you obedient without question? Or do you critically think and include your values in making a decision? Where and to what extent does your obedience lie? Gather as much information as necessary to provide the proper knowledge needed to make your decisions. In society, elites are taking more power upon themselves than *we, the people,* ever gave them. Be prepared to perform detailed research before ever blindly obeying an authority that lies opposite your values. How can you prepare for times like this? How does obedience affect your decision-making process?

12. *Need- or desire-based.* Do you allow a need or desire to compromise your decisions? Will you go against your beliefs to

satisfy a need? What about a desire? Are you willing to alter a decision and go against your values in order to attain an object in need or one you *want*? Perhaps there are some you would and some you would not. How would you handle these types of situations? What are some of your strong needs or desires? How do you evaluate their importance compared to your values? Do you consider your values and make a logical decision? Do you have control over your wants and needs? If not, what can you do to gain control over them? How will you compare opposing sides and evaluate these situations in an unbiased manner? How do your needs and desires affect your decision-making process?

13. *Insecurity.* There are many forms of insecurities that have the potential to influence decisions. Insecurity, in general, can lead people to act in peculiar ways. Perhaps you want to be liked or accepted or don't want to stand out in a crowd, or do want to stand out as unique. Perhaps it is based on a talent or the work that you do. Have you ever let an insecurity sway a decision that you made? What was the premise of the insecurity? Who was involved? Who benefited from this decision? Is there a certain insecurity that would cause you to set aside your values? What would you do if the insecurity presented itself, even though you would not be harmed by choosing your values? Are you stronger than your insecurity? How can you find out more information regarding opposing sides of the insecurity? Collect as much information as possible, then evaluate the data. How can you work toward resolving the insecurity so it is no longer an issue? How can you prepare so an insecurity is not an issue when making decisions?

There are many different factors behind the process of making a decision. Perhaps you have encountered half or even all of the mentioned conditions at some point in your life. No matter what you are experiencing or how you approach the decision, employ critical-thinking methods before you make your ultimate decisions. Who is doing what? What seems to be the reason for this happening? What are the potential or desired end results? How could they possibly change? Who does this benefit? Does the source of this information appear to have an agenda? What is the agenda? Is the source overlooking, ignoring, or leaving out information that doesn't support its beliefs or claims? Is the source using unnecessary language to sway an audience's perception of a fact? How are your values affected? What would it look like through the eyes of the opposing side? How can you meet them in the middle with a compromise and without bending your values? What are other potential responses? Is there anything clouding your judgment? Are you seeing the situation through unbiased eyes? Are you allowing other people or things to affect your decision? Are you using logic? Utilizing credible and reliable resources, research and gather as much relevant information as possible. Analyze and extrapolate your own conclusions based on the raw data.

> *We all make choices, but in the end, our choices make us.*
>
> —Ken Levine

> *We are free to choose our paths, but we can't choose the consequences that come with them.*
>
> —Sean Covey

> *Good and evil both increase at compound interest. That is why the little decisions you and I make every day are of such infinite importance.*
>
> —C. S. Lewis

> *If, before every action, we were to begin by weighing up the consequences, thinking about them in earnest, first the immediate consequences, then the probable, then the possible, then the imaginable ones, we should never move beyond the point where our first thought brought us to a halt.*
>
> —José Saramago

 Reflect:

1. What is your primary mode of decision-making? Name factors that could affect how you make your decisions.
2. Name someone you know who practices critical thinking in decision-making opportunities. How does this process affect their decision outcomes?
3. How can you incorporate more critical thinking and less influential distractions into the decisions you make?
4. Think of a time when you allowed intimidation to affect your decision-making. How can you reframe this by critical thinking?
5. How about reputation, herd mentality, peer pressure, financial advantage, fear, emotionally charged, spiritually charged, loyalty, obedience, need- or desire-based, insecurity? How can you reframe each of these methods through critical thinking?

CHAPTER 5

Why Identify?

Let me begin by saying this chapter is meant in no way to place judgment upon anyone but rather to apply critical thinking methods regarding the desire to have a label to *identify* placed on yourself, whatever that label may be. In society today, some people have become enraptured with labeling themselves with one aspect of their being. Why has it become so important to pick out one of many attributes and tag themselves with that regard? Everyone is beautifully and wonderfully made. We have talents, ambitions, gifts, and magnificent abilities. Why is there a strong desire to overlook a multitude of endearing and even impressive qualities just to focus on a decision to think of a particular thought and label oneself with this *identity*? And more importantly, how did this become a *movement* and take flight to the point that our very own government now finds it necessary to create mandates regarding this desire to highlight one aspect in people?

How did you respond when you were younger and asked what you wanted to be when you grew up? Did you respond, "I want to be known and make my mark on this world, not for my talents, abilities, or character but because I chose to have a certain type of preference"? Or did you have more talent-driven ambitions, such as being an engineer or an athlete? Or maybe a firefighter or a doctor? Or perhaps a baker, geologist, or business owner of your own makings? At what point was the decision made to choose your identity to be based on one thought or one preference?

How has society capitalized on the concept of defining yourself based on a thought or preference? How is it that businesses now require continuing education or competencies to occur and be stored in personnel files for documentation regarding preference *training*? What about focusing on the safety of our children or our country? Could infrastructure be an important thing to focus on instead? How about the importance of a standard of conduct in companies so employees are treated decently and are acknowledged for hard work and talent? How about analyzing a company's termination policies? How are businesses forced to become more concerned about a thought or *preference* than if someone is skillfully qualified to perform their job description? How did this happen? Because I prefer to put my left shoe on before my right shoe, is this how I should choose to identify myself? I believe I am of more value than labeling myself based on one thought of how I prefer to perform an act. Would a new competency be created that all employees will be mandated to perform based on which-shoe-first preference? More importantly, what can be done to refocus on priorities, and what would be the most efficient and productive manner of operation? Certainly, there must be a way that everyone can still be their own individual yet not feel a need to define themselves by a single element and then *force* their preferences into mandates, changing how businesses operate. Why is there an increasing need to identify in *any* way in the first place?

Employees and employers are being forced to *favor* people with different thoughts or preferences. What does that have to do with work? What is the basis of how this relates to work productivity and successful accomplishment? What about innocent children who should focus on a playful childhood rather than on *preferences?* This pressure has nothing to do with the child and everything to do with adults forcing the idea upon them. What is the reason for encouraging children, whose minds are not fully developed, to have to identify themselves in the first place? As a matter of fact, on average, the brain is not fully developed until approximately age twenty-five. Is it even logical to ignore this fact?

Why would businesses be forced to focus on how a person identifies rather than the abilities of the employees? What does the workplace or any place of business or public gathering have to do with a focused look at a preference? For example, it is contradictory to have sexual harassment competencies yet force everyone to focus on their *sexual identity* and give special consideration to people who choose to make that the focus of their being rather than anything work-, skill-, or character-related. Will they eventually give special consideration to people who prefer to put a shoe on their left foot first and develop competencies for this preference?

The other day, I called a new eye doctor to set up an appointment for what I considered to be a concern for my eyes. There was a very nice woman on the other end of the line. She asked logical questions and gathered important information. Then she asked me, "How do you identify?" Identify? I said, "Well, I am a person noticing some blurriness and potentially even some double vision." That wasn't the information she was looking for. I was seeking help with my vision, yet she wanted to discuss my view of *sexual* preference. How is this even logical? Was her knowledge of my views going to better help my vision? Would it serve to verify the health of my eyes? Should I have mentioned my left-foot-first shoe preference? What is the basis or logic for asking this question? Where does it ultimately stem from? And why is society laying down a red carpet to oblige a need to label someone with an *identity*? Speaking from a critical-thinking point of view, it defied logic.

Potential reasons someone might feel a need to distinctly define themselves with a type of identity

1. *Insecurity.* We all have had some form of insecurity in our lives, which is part of our human nature. What are some that come to your mind that you endured yet overcame? Was it a long process? How did you strategically overcome this obstacle? Did you use reason and logic to make sense of the obstacle? Are there any insecurities you can think of that still linger? How does a sense of insecurity present itself

to you? How do you respond to the situation when you are made aware of it? Who or what are the potential sources of the insecurity? Is it generally from words that were spoken or from an event that may or may not have happened? What are other alternatives to try to work through insecurities and bring them to a resolution? Have you ever looked at the opposing side of the insecurity, if there is one? How could seeing an alternate version affect your perspective? What type of research did you perform to understand the source of the problem? How can you research authentically and factually while showing no emotional bias? Did you resolve it within your own means? Could there be some underlying insecurity causing the desire to express to the world a particular way to define yourself? What are the talents and abilities that you have been blessed with? How are you utilizing these skills productively in your life? What if you defined yourself based on a different aspect? How many attributes can you think of to define yourself? What would change if you chose a different one? What if you placed all definitions aside and allowed yourself to be considered a worthy individual who is good just as you are, without a label? Discover the source of the insecurity using reason and logic. Make an intentional effort to uncover the source, and use skills and any necessary help to work through and heal the insecurity, leaving you better able to enjoy a content and fulfilled life.

2. *Herd mentality.* Many things are easier when you are in the comfort and security of a group. As mentioned earlier, there is strength in numbers. Often, there is a combined sharing of different perspectives, leading to productive solutions. As many come together with the same desire to *feel* accepted, it becomes easier to build strength in almost anything. Is the idea of acceptance from like-minded people causing more people to join a bandwagon? Is there comfort or a *feeling* of acceptance if you join in and align with others? Have you taken time to think about why this

has happened? Is there a sense of obligation while in the presence of the group? Are you permitted to think critically for yourself and reach your own conclusions without fear of reprisal of some sort? Sometimes, in a group setting, people can slip into the role of a follower, losing their *true* identity as an individual. Do you allow others to think for themselves without prejudice, respecting potentially different views? Can you still be yourself, despite potential persuasion, due to a group mentality? Are you highlighting your best characteristic? What are some of your other characteristics? Or are you just following a crowd? Do you find security under the umbrella of a group? What do you see as the benefit derived from a group? Would there be a bigger benefit from being away from the influence of the group? How would this be different? What factors have you considered in reaching your conclusion? Is there a chance you have given up your individual freedom for conformity?

3. *Desire for attention.* It can be difficult always to be in the background or to be shy and *feel* like you are unnoticed. Everyone appreciates at least a little attention at some point. Perhaps the desire to be seen and recognized for something is a reason for taking a defined outlook on life. Do you want to be noticed by people and catch their attention? Whom would you like to be noticed by? Have you thought about different ways to reach people that might be captivating? In what ways have you tried to get involved? What other ways can you reach out and be noticed based on abilities or accomplishments? What would be the benefit of this? How are you impacted when you are noticed? How about when you are overlooked? Is this the best decision you reached in regard to gaining some form of attention? What other forms of engagement might be endearing? What may have happened in your past that led you to be subdued? What type of research might support the idea of drawing attention to yourself? Is defining yourself by choosing an identity satisfying your desire? If so, in what ways does this

further your goals or values? What other attributes, characteristics, or actions might there be for being noticed? What type of attention might win the hearts of people without biasing others?

4. *Peer pressure.* Peer pressure is a powerful force everyone has probably experienced at one point or another in their lives. While it could be a positive or negative force, it is generally considered negative as it implies that your ability or opportunity to control your own decisions is actually influenced and *controlled by* someone else. Are you being pressured to act in a certain way? Who might be putting unwarranted pressure on you? What would the basis of this pressure be? Who would benefit from following suit with this pressure? Do you put pressure on yourself to act or be a certain way? Has someone allowed you to feel the need to take a stand and narrow the way in which you see yourself? Was there a time in your life when you clearly felt pressured by your peers? What were the surrounding circumstances? How did you respond to this situation? What are other ways you could have responded to the situation? Were you able to remain strong and *not* allow yourself to be persuaded by others? What other thoughts do you have about peer pressure? Learn to recognize if someone is attempting to snatch your power away from you by pressuring you to think or act like them. Be aware at all times of the possibility of someone or something trying to *take control* of your freedom and individuality. It can happen in the subtlest of ways. Make an effort to see the situation from an opposing perspective, then evaluate your information in an unbiased manner. Question and discover more about the motives or agendas of others in persuasive situations. Ask yourself who benefits by giving up your control, then draw your own independent conclusion without pressure from others.

5. *Emotionally charged.* It can be very difficult to think straight when those around you are emotionally charged. It may even be a little or a lot intimidating! How about the

way you make decisions when *your* emotions are running on the high side? What do you do to calm down and critically think about the situation? Has a highly emotional state, either yours or someone else's, been the driving force in *feeling* the desire to label yourself? Emotions can be powerful yet may cloud the ability to think rationally. It is not hard to get caught up in an emotionally driven cause or event. The influence can be formidable, as emotion may lead to unpredictability. What is the basis for your decision-making choices? How do emotions typically affect you? Can you think of a time when emotions clouded your decisions? What were the results of the situation? Who was involved and benefitted from the emotional stance? How about a time when you overcame an emotional situation by resolving it rationally? What steps did you take for this to occur? Are there other areas of your life driven by emotions? How do you evaluate and handle emotional situations? What is your particular way to unwind or cope when emotions are involved? What is your source of replenishing calmness in your immediate environment? How can you gain more control over your emotions?

6. *Hurt*. We have *all* been hurt in one way or another in our lifetimes. *No one* leaves this world unscathed. It is almost *guaranteed* that we will be hurt again. The way pain is afflicted is different for every person. Yet not everyone *feels* the need to react publicly. Some call it *oppression* and seek revenge. Others focus on healing themselves and building stronger, empowering, and uplifting qualities within themselves, transforming their negative energy into positive vibrations and pouring it out toward successful personal or professional development. How do you handle mentally painful situations that occurred through no fault of your own? How about physically painful situations? How about a hurtful situation you may have caused, even if it was by accident? Do you let a *historically* painful event, unexperienced by you personally, *control you* and how you respond

today? Do you let the pain *define* who you are and how you act or react? How would lashing out solve anything? Who benefits from being *reactive* rather than *proactive*? Do you understand that *everyone* has had some form of pain in their lives, not simply you? While it is very unfortunate that you are hurting, what are better methods to heal, remove the pain, and *move forward peacefully* rather than allow yourself to be *controlled* by it? A *choice* can be made to find the source of the pain. Address it in a healthy, positive, and joy-filled way, and actually alleviate the hurt permanently! Have you taken the time to see things from an opposing perspective? Do you choose to be influenced by the pressure of others, or are you *unwilling* to act based on emotion and pressure? How do you evaluate the source of the hurt? What methods do you undergo to heal? How can you alter any negative responses regarding the source of the pain? What do you know about the source of the pain? Who or what is the cause? What is your desired outcome of choosing an identity derived from a hurt? Does this permanently resolve the problem without harming or focusing on anyone else in the process, allowing contentment and productivity to prevail? What outcome do you extrapolate from a certain tag? Are you able to let go of bitterness and forgive? Or do you hold on to the bitterness, let it *control* you, and use it to inflame someone else? How can you *choose* to let go of the hurt and regain your control?

Think of numerous methods that involve your healing *without* further hurt inflicted upon anyone else. In my book, *Elevate Your Mind to Success*, this is what I call *"successfully revenged."* All of the energy and passion from the painful event is focused on your ability to become *massively successful* and highly prosperous while *removing* the source of hurt from your mind. You are taught how to reprogram your mind to automatically focus on success and positive and empowering energy. As long as you let hurtful sources *control* your mind and continue to focus on them, they continue to win, no matter what you do. Let them go *completely* and focus on leading a successful, bitter-free, and joyful life unaffected by the negativity of others or thoughts from the past. How would focusing on healing and building positive and fruitful energy in your own life change your perspective? How would your health and outlook benefit from healing your heart *and* mind? Has your method of resolving a hurtful event ever involved meditation or prayer? Who is a close friend who will listen without prejudice? How can you *be* this kind of friend to others? How can you not let pain define and control you? Consider ways you can hold on to your freedom to think as an individual rather than conforming to the guise of others.

7. *Sensitized.* Many things and people are becoming more and more sensitized today. People *choose* to allow their *feelings* to be hurt at the slightest sign of discomfort. Lately, people have been taking things quite personally and becoming *offended* at the slightest verbiage. How are you *sensitized* by things people say? What can you do not to allow cruel words to affect you personally? Being *offended* is a *choice*. The one offended has now *made it* their problem too. How can you evaluate the truth or falsehood of the words they say? Perhaps the other person is hurting and does not know how to process their feelings, so they *take it out* on you. How can you be aware when this occurs? What can you do to instinctively *critically think* about what they have just said and done so you can reveal the truth behind the words or the event?

Do you become *emotional* if things aren't exactly as you would like them to be? Or are you able to be *tolerant* and forgiving? How can you become more tolerant and forgiving? How could you benefit from becoming this way? Do you stop and think about both sides of a situation? Or are you quick to react, taking things personally or responding like water off a duck's back, sensing a deeper, underlying issue with the *other* person, and the problem is actually *their* problem? How can you become more confident and think critically rather than *feeling* or actually becoming sensitized? Perhaps you could focus on enjoying the world a little more and taking people's actions a little less seriously. How skilled are you at practicing patience and extending grace to others? These can both be *very* challenging skills to perform! Yet both are *extremely admirable* qualities to encompass. Both would be incredible qualities to identify as, if you must identify at all. Would you like patience, grace, and forgiveness extended to you when you were at fault or needed compassion? Realize that feelings are a choice you make based on the programming of your thoughts. They do not define you, nor is it wise to base your actions on them. They are *unreliable* and *subject to change circumstantially.* Reprogram your mind with solid, objective thoughts that you choose, aligned with your values, and embed them in your mind with your own individually selected program, as defined in *Elevate Your Mind to Success.* Allow this programming to produce automatic, *logical* responses that parallel your belief system and provide contentedness in your daily life. You will never regret a decision made based on logic. However, a decision based on *feelings* is subject to change based on the situation and can lead to long-lasting regret.

8. *To counter shame or guilt.* We have all done things in life that we may feel shameful for or maybe ridden with guilt. I certainly hope I am not just speaking for myself! There are so many life lessons to be learned. Some people (like me) generally end up learning the hard way! Think of a time or event when you felt ashamed of something you did or said. How about when you felt guilty? How did you respond or react during any of these circumstances? Would you react the same way today if another similar situation occurred? How might you respond differently? Have you ever let guilt or shame influence you into doing something boldly

to overcome the negative feelings that were attached? How can you critically think about the basis of guilt or shame in an unbiased manner? Is there a link between past treatment you endured and a new desire to define yourself? How can this be an effective way to resolve those *feelings*? What other alternatives can you think of to create a new vision of an unfortunate occurrence? How can you heal feelings of guilt or shame so you can react on the basis of *logic* and *reasoning* rather than emotion? How would this be beneficial? Consider the opposing sides of healing versus reacting. Does an attempt to change other people's perspectives change how you view yourself? How are you affected by how others see you? Think about ways to productively heal unfavorable *feelings* from the past and move forward peacefully and *logically* without pressure to react.

9. *Pride.* Pride is said to be one of the most destructive and dangerous qualities. There is a good pride and a bad pride. It is good to be proud of your children or perhaps even your accomplishments or abilities. A positive and upbeat implication is attached to this pride, positively affecting others. The other type of pride carries with it negativity and destructive properties. It is evil-based and *self-serving*. This type of pride is restrictive, condescending, and poisonous and carries with it the potential or even desire to hurt someone else or prove something. To understand which sense of pride is in effect, ask yourself critical-thinking questions. What or who is the source of your pride? What type of energy is attached to the pride, negative or positive vibrations? What is the desired outcome in response to the pride? Does it stem from a place of hurt and pain or a place of joy, contentment, and encouragement? What is the reason for the pride? What is your source of information in the circumstance? Is the intent either to help someone or hurt someone? Set aside your own personal bias and evaluate the claim. Look at it from different viewpoints. What conclusions do you draw based on the information you

collected? What do you think is going on? What information is most important in your determination? How do you know you have all the information? What is your direction in the position you have chosen? How might the stance you are taking affect other people? How do you intend for them to be affected? Analyze your motives, if they are present, and determine your reason for engaging them. Could pride be clouding your judgment in any way? How do you determine the answer to that? If unhealthy pride is involved, how can you address these feelings and reprogram your thoughts to positive and uplifting ones? Beware of any prideful tendencies, and use logic to reason through the circumstances involved.

Take some time to critically think about the source of the desire to have a defined identity. Or perhaps consider why someone else might be led to this desire. What seems to be the underlying reason for this happening? What or who has led to this decision? What is the expected or at least desired outcome? What are the benefits that are linked to having a label? What are the benefits without it? How can you independently establish this decision without influence from anyone else? How would you describe the emotion that is attached to the decision to define yourself? How can you reevaluate the situation, take your own personal bias out, and see things from other vantage points? Is your decision full of positive or negative energy? How can you make it all positive-energy based? What is it that you truly want to be known for? Do you want to be defined by a thought or an action? Or what about by an ability? Or perhaps an act of service to others? How would you like your obituary to read if available to be seen for generations to come? What words of description would you like to be on your tombstone engraved permanently? Is there still a desire to identify as anything? Have you thought of other qualities you possess that would define you better, leaving you feeling uplifted or enlightened? Critically think about the idea of identifying yourself. Think of the pros, cons, and reasons involved. Also, think about why you would choose a certain tag. Consider your answers, opposing answers, and other alternatives from an unbiased perspective. Where does this lead your thoughts?

> *There will always be someone willing to hurt you, put you down, gossip about you, belittle your accomplishments and judge your soul. It is a fact that we all must face. However, if you realize that God is a best friend that stands beside you when others cast stones, you will never be afraid, never feel worthless and never feel alone.*
> —Shannon Alder

> *There are moments when troubles enter our lives and we can do nothing to avoid them. But they are there for a reason. Only when we have overcome them will we understand why they were there.*
> —Paulo Coelho

> *Every second you dwell on the past you steal from your future. Every minute you spend focusing on your problems you take away from finding your solutions.*
> —Robin Sharma

> *I've learned that people will forget what you said, people will forget what you did, but people will never forget how you made them feel.*
> —Maya Angelou

> *Let your hopes, not your hurts, shape your future.*
> —Robert H. Schuller

Reflect:

1. Are you a person who finds it necessary to define yourself? If so, how do you define yourself?
2. What is the basis or driving factor that leads you to this position? Is there positive or negative energy involved?
3. How do you allow *feelings* to affect your decisions? In what ways can feelings be unreliable?
4. How do you allow *logic* and *reasoning* to affect your decisions?
5. How have events in your past influenced who you are at this very moment?
6. Think about how you would like to be thought of in years to come. Is your current stance in line with your desired legacy? Are there any changes you would like to make?
7. Write out what you would like your obituary to say. What is your desired legacy? What steps do you need to take to lay the foundation for this legacy?

CHAPTER 6

Who's to Blame?

Have you noticed there is more finger-pointing in the world around you today than ever before? Very few, or perhaps almost no one, seem to be at fault for all the issues around you professionally and personally, yet everyone is blaming *everyone else* as the one at fault. Taking responsibility for one's own actions is becoming a rare occurrence, yet it is a highly regarded and impressive attribute to encompass. Blame is a claim that someone other than yourself is responsible for a certain act, cause, situation, or lately, even a *feeling* one experiences. There are even *movements* occurring based on the *belief* that *it* was someone else's fault. If you have ever met or owned your own teenager, you know exactly about the blame game. Nothing is ever their fault! But it is time to critically think about the concept of partaking in this same action of blaming others and looking at the *actual* source, leading to this potential action.

I once worked for a company that was run by an unqualified management staff that promoted employees to a higher rank based on whoever was willing to accept the position when an opening presented itself. My own boss, as a matter of fact, had a criminal record and never held a management position before but was the only one at that time who was willing and had the required license available, so she received the position and title with no additional management skill training. In this same company, all employees were required to hold a current CPR certification, yet the word around the workplace was that if something happened to a patient, you were not permitted to perform CPR on them. Using my critical thinking skills, I asked myself, "Why would we be required to hold an active certification if we were not permitted to use the skills to potentially save a life?" It appeared to be an illogical process. So, I asked around to random employees and consistently received the same response from *every* one of them, "I don't know." I then contacted the head of the education department and asked this very same question. I received a disappointing, surprising, and extremely unhelpful response. Quite defensively, she asked, "Where did you hear that? Who said this? Give me a specific name right now. Who was it?" Wow. Such a defensive stance was taken that in no way helped to find a resolution to the question I had presented. How would finding out *who* (which was actually *everyone* I had asked) help bring the issue closer to resolution? How would giving names of those who did not know provide an answer to whether or not the act of CPR was permitted to occur? What was the premise of asking these questions? Was there a deficiency in the education department in relaying critical information? Was the response a personal agenda? Why was this person seeking a name in which to blame rather than focusing on a solution? How would knowing a name in which to place blame begin the process of educating the employees on a procedure that was confusing to the *entire* staff for what appeared to be a *very* long time?

Reasons why people choose to blame others

1. *Fear.* Fear covers a large array of territory, including some of the bullet points that follow. *False events appearing real* is a crippling *feeling* that causes people to do or say unfortunate or unnecessary things. What is the fear? Is there fear of reprisal for not performing the duties of a job or fear of *feeling* inadequate? Where does the fear stem from? What is the worst-case scenario if the fear comes to fruition? Recalling that a fear is something that has *not actually happened*, what are possible situations that may occur? How likely are they to occur? What evaluation can be per-

formed to shed light on alternatives? Who is involved with this fear? What result is desired from choosing to blame others in a situation based on a fear? What ways could be chosen to be more productive? What if the choice could be made to focus on a *solution* rather than a fear? What could this possibly hurt? Or could it be helpful? How could the fear be overcome? What methods are currently being used? How can all bias be taken out of a scenario in order to find a productive solution rather than blame someone? What if the situation was in reverse? How would you handle unwarranted blame due to a fear being placed on you? How can you create a situation with positive energy where it becomes instinctive to seek solutions rather than choose a defensive stance? How could this improve the environment around you? How would this change your workplace atmosphere? How can you identify fears, reason them out, and eliminate them?

2. *Guilt.* Guilt may leave an empty and anxious *feeling* looming inside. Guilt could lead to blaming someone else for something that occurred, with the possible result of *temporarily* relieving the anxiety. What is the basis of the guilt? Where does it stem from? What are the circumstances that surround the situation? How can the guilt be resolved in an unbiased way within your own means? What have you learned from the situation? How would you respond differently next time? What would the premise be of blaming someone else for an issue due to feelings of guilt? What are other ways that the situation could be dealt with without blaming someone else? What is the truth in the situation? How do you handle *feelings* of guilt? Is there a need to step back and resolve any situations of guilt? How has this shaped your decisions? How can logic and reasoning be utilized in reframing the guilt? What conclusions can you draw for an effective resolution?

3. *Pride.* Could the *hurtful* type of pride, as discussed in the previous chapter, be a reason for choosing to blame some-

one else? What are the surrounding circumstances of the pride? How did the situation of blame arise? What are some alternate ways to respond rather than blaming someone else? Who is involved in the circumstance involving pride? What is a response that could lead to a productive outcome? Evaluate the situation. What are all of the circumstances that have led to the response? How did the response fit the evaluated information? What is the desired outcome of the reaction? How can the pride be addressed in order to resolve the negative feelings attached to it? Often, a temporary *good* feeling will still leave you empty or hurting inside once again as the issue itself has not been resolved, such as if the feelings were reframed and properly healed. How can you decipher the source of the pride? How can you heal negative feelings so there is a lasting resolution? What if you tried to *resolve* the source in order to heal rather than react and rebuke?

4. *Hurt.* Hurt can lead to a multitude of responses, one of which can be to *lash out* and blame someone else. Has someone who was hurting ever lashed out and blamed you for something? How did you handle this situation? Was this ever a pathway you chose? Who was involved in this interaction? How did this resolve the issue? Have you ever allowed hurt to be a reason to blame someone for something? How do you rationalize this decision? What type of research was performed before you made this decision? What is the basis of the decision? What other options for resolution are there? How could you respond differently? What would happen if you resolved the hurt feelings first? What alternative approaches could you take to handle the situation? Have you ever had a successful outcome by blaming someone else? Have you viewed the situation from an opposing perspective? How did you choose the person you picked to blame? How did they hurt you? How will you *logically* move past the hurt?

5. *Insecurity.* Have you ever blamed someone due to an insecurity you had or have? Who was involved in the circumstance? What role did they play? What were the circumstances that led to this decision? What research did you perform to reach the decision on which to act? What are some alternate choices that could've been made? What is the insecurity? How has this affected your life? What steps have you taken in an attempt to eliminate the insecurity? How did you evaluate the steps it would take? Who could help with the source of the insecurity? How did you justify your responses? Would you choose a different way to respond? How has an insecurity caused you to respond in other circumstances? Have you been able to find a way to take control of the insecurity? How will you logically resolve the insecurity?

6. *Peer pressure.* Peer pressure is a consistent and repetitious force that will always be a contention in our lives. Have you ever allowed pressure from someone else to cause you to blame another person for something? How did you reach a decision to do this? Who was involved in the circumstance? Were they actually guilty or not? How did you respond when the decision was made? What would have been an alternate way to respond? How often do you hand over control to someone else due to pressure? How can you be more aware when you are being pressured and step back to critically think about the situation from an unbiased perspective? Have you ever been the recipient of blame due to a peer pressure situation? How was it resolved? How can you overcome the influence of someone else and make your own decisions?

7. *Irresponsibility.* Everyone has been brought up differently and under differing circumstances. What were your circumstances like? What type of emphasis was placed on being responsible? Who was involved in developing your character? How much emphasis was placed on this development? Have you ever blamed someone in order to *dodge*

responsibility? What are ways in which this could happen? How could it be prevented? What are ways you can develop the character quality of being responsible? How can you take responsibility for your actions? How are others affected if you aren't responsible for your actions? What benefits are involved with being responsible? What consequences might occur if you did *not* take responsibility for your actions? How do the people that surround you respond when the responsibility is theirs? What would happen if you made this a steadfast quality in your life? What could the benefits be?

8. *Unaccountability.* Have you ever been in a situation where someone was not accountable for their actions and it negatively affected you? Who was involved? How did you respond? What were the consequences? Has there been a time when you were not accountable for your actions? Have you ever blamed someone when the accountability was actually your responsibility? What were the circumstances surrounding this event? Who was involved? How was the recipient affected by your decision? What are other ways you could have responded? What are some possible different outcomes? How can you evaluate each of these scenarios? How could the situation have been handled better? How can you be more accountable for your actions and your words? It's important to be accountable for yourself. It takes integrity and an authentic person to accept accountability for *all* of the actions that are chosen by you. How can you program this quality into your mind so it becomes an instinctive response?

9. *Reputation.* Sometimes, to spare a reputation, people may choose to blame someone else for something they have done. Has this ever happened to you? Has someone ever blamed you for something they did in order to protect their reputation? How did you handle the situation? Have you ever blamed someone else for something to protect *your* reputation? In either case, what was the outcome? Who was

involved in the blame? What are some better alternatives regarding how the situation could have been addressed? How do you wish you had responded? In what ways could the result be positive for both sides? How did you find yourself in the predicament to begin with? How was the other person affected? In what ways can you avoid a future occurrence like this? What have you learned about the situation?

10. *Uneducated or uninformed.* Lack of education can be an element leading to blame. Have you ever been blamed by someone who didn't fully understand a situation? How about the reverse circumstance? Have you ever blamed someone else before you had all of the facts? How did you expect the outcome to play out? How did it actually turn out? Who was involved in this circumstance? What choices could you have made differently? How many options did you entertain before you made your decision on how you responded? How much and what kind of research did you do in preparation for your action? How could you become better informed about the situation? What would you change about your responses? How can you use this information for future situations? Has education, or lack thereof, been a problem before in making decisions? How do you keep yourself current on information? Do you gather all facts from your side and the opposing side before you come to a conclusion? How can you program this type of thinking into your mind for instinctive responses?

11. *Personality types.* People with different personality types can choose certain and almost predictable responses. Narcissists, for example, are notorious for blaming anyone in their pathway for anything they can think of. They are rarely, if ever, accountable for anything. It seems they are *never* wrong about anything *in their eyes*. There are other toxic personality types that respond the same way. Be aware of who you are involved with and the potential for blame against you that may occur. How could a blame scenario

with toxic personality types be avoided? What steps could you take to protect yourself? How much do you know about toxic personality types? Do you have one of these personalities? How would you respond in either case? How can you focus on the facts at hand and allow them to be the focus of the responses using an unbiased perspective? What education might be helpful to learn more about this topic? How do you recognize this type of personality type?

12. *Shame.* Have you ever been on the receiving end of blame, involving shame felt because of another person? How did you handle this situation? What were the surrounding circumstances? Has shame ever driven you to blame someone else for something? What would be the premise of this action? What would be the expected outcome of blaming someone else? How could it be avoided? What is the source of shame? How can that be resolved? How can the *feeling* of shame be identified, understood, and dealt with to resolution? In what ways can this be avoided in the future? What do you know about shame? How can you help someone else who *feels* a sense of shame? What information can be researched to deal with this *feeling* in a healthy way?

13. *Financial incentive.* Has a financial incentive, either profitable or costly, ever been a reason used to blame someone else? Has someone blamed you for something, with finances being the influencing factor of the blame? Money can be very influential. What are ways you could see money affecting people? How might the influence of money cause someone to place blame on someone else? What might be the expected outcome? How can you ensure money is never used as an excuse to blame someone else? What would be the benefits of securing a plan? Do you know anyone who placed blame on someone else due to a monetary matter? How did the matter transpire? How could this have been better handled? What are the possible outcomes for this person? What did you learn from this experience? *Follow the money.*

14. *Justification.* People are capable of many sorts of things in their pursuit to justify themselves or their actions. Has anyone ever blamed you for something for the sake of their justification? Have you ever blamed someone else in order to justify something? Who was involved? What was the premise of the need to justify? What was the expected outcome of blaming someone else? Was the desired result received? What other choices could have been made? How would a change in previous decisions change the outcome? What could be done differently? Was the issue that needed to be resolved ever properly accounted for? What can be learned from this situation?

Blame is more and more common in all facets of life. It is even occurring based on historical events that are not even in existence today. What might be the reasons someone would place blame for something that occurred in the past? How would a past event not brought on by *any* people currently today be a reason to place fault on someone today? What reasoning is used to justify blame for events of the past in the current setting? How might this situation look to the ones that are being blamed that also were not in the past events? How are they, or are they not, really at fault? How does it look if the situation was evaluated from the opposing side? What evidence is there to link today's people with the actions of the past? What is the expected outcome of the action of blaming? What is the premise of the action? What has led to this action? What can be learned from history? How does blaming a historical event on current events today change anything? Does erasing the past make the events not real anymore? Or did they still really happen? What are alternative ways to handle the situation? What is a more productive response that can lead to a supportive and favorable current or future perspective? How can this be positively applied to your lifestyle today? Are you able to learn and grow because of it? How can you resolve any potential negative feelings and transform the energy into positive and productive energy?

Blame is an ineffective way to resolve any situation. It is a defensive stance that is counterintuitive to a resolution. How can you find alternative ways to view a situation? What other methods can you think of to resolve hurt *feelings* due to a past or other painful situation? What are the reasons for taking it personally, even if you were *not* personally there? What might happen if you had the courage enough to accept your life choices and where you are right now? If you are unhappy with the scenario, what productive and positive changes can you make in your life to improve your situation? Without focusing on anyone else and a need to blame someone, how can you find enjoyment in life? What are your gifts and talents? How can you use them in a fun, useful, and creative way? What activities do you enjoy? What is something you have always desired to accomplish or succeed in? What would it take to pursue this dream? How can you learn more about accountability? Take responsibility for your actions. Be confident in who you are and where you are.

Learn to think for yourself without prejudice, and focus on self-improvement and making choices that lead to true and continuous joy rather than *temporary* "happiness." Blame may provide a brief satisfaction as it "justifies" a hurt, but this *temporary* happiness is subject to circumstances. At the same time, no one can take your joy away. Joy is a *sustainable* state of contentedness based on faith, hope, and security regarding what is to come, *not* based on a temporary past or current circumstantial event. Seek to *fill your life* with joy.

> *All blame is a waste of time. No matter how much fault you find with another, and regardless of how much you blame him, it will not change you. The only thing blame does is to keep the focus off you when you are looking for external reasons to explain your unhappiness or frustration. You may succeed in making another feel guilty about something by blaming him, but you won't succeed in changing whatever it is about you that is making you unhappy.*
>
> —Wayne Dyer

You can either blame everybody else or you can take a look at yourself and determine where you can improve.

—Robert Kiyosaki

If you could kick the person in the pants responsible for most of your trouble, you wouldn't sit for a month.

—Theodore Roosevelt

You will never become who you want to be if you keep blaming everyone else for who you are now.

—John Spence

You can get discouraged many times, but you are not a failure until you begin to blame somebody else and stop trying.

—John Burroughs

 Reflect:

1. Are you a person who finds it necessary to blame yourself or others? If so, what might be a better way to approach a situation?
2. What driving factor may lead you to consider blaming someone else for something you did or experienced?
3. Think of someone you know who tends to blame others. Now think of someone who takes on all their own responsibility and is always accountable for their actions. Compare and contrast the differences between the two. What do you notice?
4. Looking at two or more different sides to a story, what might be a better approach to take in a difficult situation?
5. How have events in your past influenced how you perceive blame?

6. Think about how you would like to be thought of in years to come. Is your current view regarding blame in line with your desired legacy? Are there any changes you would like to make?
7. How can you be productive and incorporate the positive character qualities of responsibility and accountability into your programming?
8. Who can you share this outlook with that may benefit from its supportive nature?
9. Critically think about the concept of blame. What comes to mind?

CHAPTER 7

Why All the Propaganda?

What is the purpose of propaganda, and where did it all begin? Propaganda has become a powerful tool used to gain approval. It is a way to sway the masses through all available media sources by those in a position to do so, including the military! While the origins of its inception were innocent enough back in 1622, according to Edward Bernays in his book *Propaganda*, it has now evolved into an entity of "troubling connotation" as it has become a method of *manipulation* and intended enterprise.[4] Propaganda is used today as a method of *controlling* how *you* think and act.

In 2013, the president of the United States signed the Smith-Mundt Modernization Act of 2012 into law, which was part of the 2013 National Defense Authorization Act, which in essence, *legalized lying* to the public for propaganda purposes.[5]

> *Today, the military is more focused on manipulating news and commentary on the internet, especially social media, by posting material and images without necessarily claiming ownership.*

From that day forward, news and journalist reporting became *no longer required* to be factual. This is all befitting George Orwell's literary work, *Nineteen Eighty-Four*. The American people are now being propagandized by the US government through many forms, including via control of major media outlets, Big Pharma, social media, and tech giants, to name a few. Take some time to read sources such as *Propaganda*, *Nineteen Eighty-Four*, *Animal Farm*, *United States of Fear*, the Smith-Mundt Modernization Act, *Turtles All the Way Down*,[6] and many other sources of your own choosing.

While you may have already noticed the media not relaying factual content, were you aware that they have been given *permission* and have even been encouraged to *deliberately deceive* you? Apply critical-thinking methods to this topic. Who is involved in the deception? What is the agenda of the deception? Who will benefit from the deception? What are the underlying reasons for the deception? Why would a law have been passed to allow government sources to lie to the American people? What is their perspective regarding this topic? Do they have *your* best interests in mind? What is your perspective on this topic? What is your response to the permission to deceive in order to persuade you? How does this affect you? How will this configure your thoughts as you listen to the media outlets from now on? Will you apply critical-thinking questions to each piece of media you encounter? What current practices will you change in response to this knowledge? How are you affected by manipulative information? How have they been effective in convincing you to believe in their content? What methods do you apply to verify the legitimacy of the content? How do you know the truth behind the content? Will you think differently regarding their information? How can you better prepare to handle more and more media outlets as they conform to the freedom to deceive? Knowing they intend to *control* you, how will you respond? Will you allow them to control you and connect your dots for you? Or will you take steps of awareness and program your mind to automatically *question the intent* of the content? It is important to arm yourself with the necessary information based on your decision. What research will you do to verify sources and content? Be careful and methodical as you analyze your research. It is helpful to understand how manipulation is used.

Keys to successful manipulation

1. *Utilizing and controlling appropriate media outlets.* The government and other political venues have successfully gained control of nearly all major news and media outlets. This was not an accidental occurrence. And it was also not a sudden occurrence. When did you come to an awareness that this was happening? Who owns the different outlets? What are the connections among the owners? What is the agenda of having a monopoly over major media sources? What are the possible outcomes of the monopoly? How could or does this affect you? What conclusion do you come to regarding this movement of control? What are the possible benefits of total control? What are the disadvantages of complete control? Who are they trying to manipulate? What seems to be the reason for the manipulation? What are the desired end results of doing this? How could this change things? How does *any* monopoly have positive outcomes? Whom does the manipulation benefit? Does the source of the media outlets appear to have an agenda regarding the manipulation? Are they overlooking, ignoring, or leaving out information that doesn't support its agenda? Are they using unnecessary persuasive language to sway the audience's perception of a fact? How will you research the content provided? How will you verify the validity of the information? Ensure you seek the most relevant information as you collect as much data as possible. Evaluate all of the raw data, and extrapolate potential outcomes. Draw your own conclusion. Do you realize you are not as *free* as you once thought?

2. *Taking away the individual.* The government is trying desperately and is succeeding, in manipulating people into forming groups and having a group mentality. They are *afraid* to have people think and act individually and be a strong force of their own with their own thoughts, agenda, and individual actions. People can be compelling when they

use their own logic and intellect, so powerful, in fact, that they are feared. Thus, movements have been well underway to promote groups of people, encouraging them to pick an identity or, in some way, be a part of a group and engage in emotional bonds to keep their focus on that group rather than realizing *individual* rights are being absorbed by the government, thereby *weakening* the "people" as a whole. *They* are *dividing* us. Being a part of a group is not a concern until it becomes focused on an *emotional* endeavor, giving more and more power to the *governing body* rather than to the rights of the *individual.* It is all a *loss of control* for the people and *more strength* for the government. Who is in charge of promoting groupthink? What seems to be the reason for this happening? What appears to be the desired end results of groupthink? How could this change things? Who does this benefit? Does the source of this information appear to have an underlying agenda? Is the agenda to help, nourish, encourage, and grow you? Is the source overlooking, ignoring, or leaving out information that doesn't support its agenda? Is the source using unnecessary persuasive language to sway your perception of a fact? What research can be performed from a neutral and unbiased source to find more information? What would the result be of weakening the unity of the people as a whole? How can we all still be our own individuals yet stand *together* as *individuals* and *strengthen each other* as a country rather than *hand over control* to the government? What would the benefits be if we could all be ourselves as individuals and support each other yet not give over our control to the government? What if we relinquished group thinking and used our own *individual* power and ability to critically think and analyze situations with the goal of a *stronger and unified* country?

3. *Developing fear in people.* Fear is the *primary* way to gain *control over* people. When people *feel* afraid or are in harm, they bow down to authority quickly. Look how easy it was to create a worldwide stir and make people *want* to stay

home and wear masks, even while alone in a desolate place. Fear is the only way to create a movement on such a large scale. Can you think of any way to make people *willingly* concede to having spiked protein factories injected into them and, in some cases, two, three, four, and even five times? What research has been done to learn more about the source of the "virus"? How about the experimental vaccine? Have you found evidence proving the virus has actually been around for quite a while *prior* to the claim? What news outlet did you gather information about it from upon discovering it? Was the information you collected from a major news outlet that has permission and encouragement to *deceive*? How effective were the volatile words (*urgent, critical, deadly, pandemic*) at achieving the desired effect, gaining *control* over people? Who is stirring up fear? How effective is fear in forcing people to do something? What seems to be the underlying reason for this happening? What appears to be the desired end result of the fear? How could this change things? Whom does the fear benefit? Is there some sort of funding involved or a financial incentive? Does the source of this information appear to have an agenda? Is the source overlooking, ignoring, or leaving out information that doesn't support its agenda? Has anyone been censored if they shared an opposing view? Is the source using unnecessary and persuasive language to sway the audience's perception of the facts? Was the media "fair and unbiased"? Where can you go to find scientific evidence? What information can morticians, embalmers, and funeral directors provide who have seen the *resulting evidence* of the claims and, in this case, the *experimental* "vaccine"?[7] How can you undergo unbiased research and find answers for yourself? Search for as many resources as possible from both sides of the argument. Be sure to find credible sources to discover the most relevant information regarding this data, and gather as much as possible. Use your own ability to infer and draw conclusions after evaluating all of the data.

4. *Creating a solution.* Once fear is instilled, the next step is to create a solution. For instance, as popular computer software became available decades ago, computers and systems ran amazingly well, perhaps too well. How could this be profitable? What could make it *more* profitable? How about a virus released so that more products could be created and purchased to resolve the new issue? Thus, the invention of computer viruses and yet another lucrative endeavor. How about for a human-infected virus? Then there would be a demand for a vaccine to counter the virus. Governing bodies have chosen this method of creating a problem and then creating a solution for generations. As it stands, it is extremely desirable to get any vaccine approved for the childhood list of vaccines. This is a goal of Big Pharma in order to secure *enormous* profits.[2] It then becomes a money factory. Who is creating a solution? Who is funding the research to make this possible? What seems to be the claim for the solution? What are the desired end results of the solution? How could this change things? Whom does the solution benefit? Is there extensive research proving the safety of the solution? Where can you find credible data regarding the safety of the solution? Does the source of the solution appear to have an agenda? Is there a monetary benefit to the source of the solution? Are there any alternate solutions? Who else may benefit? Is there a secondary agenda? Is the source overlooking, ignoring, falsifying, or leaving out information that does not support its claim? Is there censorship for anyone with opposing views? Is the source of the solution using persuasive language to sway people's perception of the facts? What research can you perform using valid, detailed, and unbiased sources? Where can you find reliable and the most relevant information? Always, *always* perform your own research, and

choose credible and multiple sources. Evaluate all of the information collected, and draw your own conclusions.

5. *Changing or creating laws to fit the agenda.* Just as what had occurred in 2013, a method of manipulation may be established by changing laws to fit an agenda. This could happen at any level, but people already in authority are generally the ones who have the power to do this. Sure enough, in 2013, the act was signed to allow and encourage the media to deceive the American people through propaganda. When you can force people to be subjected to certain things, there is a greater chance that submission to the influence will occur. What situation can you think of in which a law or rule was established or adjusted to fit someone else's specific agenda? Who changed the laws? What seems to be the reason for the changes? What are the desired end results of changing the law? How could this change things? Who received benefits from this occurrence? How are you affected by it? Does the source of the changed laws appear to have an agenda? What does it appear to be? Is the source stacking hidden clauses buried deep within another law to ensure its passage? Is the source overlooking, ignoring, or leaving out pertinent information that does not support its claim? Is the source using unnecessarily persuasive language to sway the people's perception of facts? How can you evaluate the situation so you understand the terms? What do you see if you look at things from the opposing perspective? How can you protect yourself from manipulation? How do you know when you are being controlled, deceived, or manipulated? Where can you find unbiased information? Gather as much data as possible from credible sources. Use your ability to infer, to discover potential conclusions.

6. *Taking control of positions of power.* In order to influence a massive amount of people, it is necessary to be in a position of power or know someone in such a position. How can a position of power give an extra advantage? Who is

the main target of interest for this position? What is the particular position? What seems to be the reason for the certain position? Is it a position of power? Who funded the campaign? What connection or involvement do they have? What or who does the position control? What appears to be the desired end result of being in the position? How could this change things? Will they be working in your favor? Who else might they be working for? What does the position have authority over? Are the policies or rules created and enforced for the best interest of the people being served? Who benefits from them being in this position? Who benefits from their decisions? How does this affect you? What appears to be the agenda of being in this position? Does there appear to be any hidden agendas? How does the source benefit from being in this position? How can you find out the intent of the actions? Are there alternate people interested in this position? Who is the best qualified for this position? Did the source resort to downplaying or humiliating their opponent in order to make themselves look better for the position? Is there any effort for deception in attaining this position? Does the source use persuasive language to sway the people's perception of the facts? What is the basis for their campaign or selection? Do extensive research for every elected official promoting something questionable. Find sources of information regarding all people running for a position of power, including opposing sides. Put aside your biases and prejudices and gather information from multiple, credible, and varying resources. Collect as much information as possible. Determine which information is most relevant, evaluate and analyze all data, extrapolate and discover facts, then draw your own conclusions without prejudice or influence from anyone else.

7. *Dependency within people.* Submission can be gained by developing a dependence within the people toward the ones in authority. This can be acquired through numerous

avenues, including via fear, group thinking, deceit from the media, etc. Successful leadership involves one in the position of authority, *serving* the needs of those who did the electing. Unfortunately, governing officials have somehow abused their power and turned the positions into *self-serving agendas* that involve manipulating the people to serve *their* needs and desires. Who is working for whom? Who is causing a dependency? Why might there be a need for the dependency? What seems to be the desired end result of the dependency? How could this change things? Who is the focus of the agenda? How can you become more independent? How does the government use the media to create a dependency within people? Who benefits from this dependency? How does this affect you? What happens if the majority of people become dependent on the government? How can you find relevant and unbiased information about this topic? Collect as much information as possible regarding dependency. Evaluate and analyze the information. Draw your own conclusions using your own unbiased logic.

8. *Creating controversy.* Did you happen to notice the real *enhanced* issue of racism, fascism, and other politically overutilized "-isms" only progressed when the first black president came into office and *promoted and exploited* this idea? Do not take my word for it; instead, do your own research and gather facts regarding this topic. If you divide the country and the people, the government becomes *stronger*, and the people become *weaker*. So many groups have fallen for this tactic and played right into the hands of the instigators. There is now more reliance *by* the people *on* the government. This is *precisely* the intent of the effort. In this sense, the government is becoming *more* powerful. Who started the instigating? What might the motives be for this movement of creating *emotional-based* controversies? Who benefits from a stronger government and weaker people? What is the desired outcome of controversy among the

people? How does the government become stronger as the people become weaker? What are the potential outcomes of this result? How does this concern you? How do you fit into this scenario? What research can you do to find out facts for clarification? What sources can you identify that will provide unbiased information? What would happen if the government and media stopped promoting the idea of these "-isms"? Collect as much data as possible. Develop an eye for unsourced claims, and consider why they are not forthcoming with the source. Where is censorship occurring? Draw your own independent conclusions from the raw data you collected. Have you noticed any of your freedoms slipping away?

9. *Destroying the family.* If there is a breakdown in the family, there is a *lack* of unity and strength in raising children under family terms. The children become elements of the court system and are immediately under *more control* of governing decisions. Each parent has a loss of rights in raising the child, and now the child can succumb more readily to the manipulation of others with an agenda that is *not* in the child's best interest. The public school system also has the freedom to manipulate children under governmental control at the lowest grade levels and has had decades plus years to program them to their agenda. How could the influence of others program the minds of children? Who is trying to destroy the family unity? What seems to be the reasoning for this? What appears to be the desired end results of this? How could this change things? Who does destroying the family unit benefit? Does the source for this breakdown appear to have an agenda? Is the source overlooking, ignoring, or leaving out information that doesn't support its beliefs? Is the source using unnecessary language to sway the people's perception of the facts? How could the breakdown of the family be detrimental to the *individual* versus the *government*? How could a strong family unit strengthen the unity within a country? How could

a strong family unit weaken the government? What effects do you see with the breakdown of the family? What type of unbiased research can be performed to find out more information? Find credible sources and gather as much information as possible. Research, then analyze all of the data collected. Formulate your own conclusions without prejudice.

10. *Destroying the churches.* Churches are a unit of strength with an image of morality or some sort of moral code. Each one may stand on its own ground and for possibly different things. Yet it is something that the government fears as it threatens their agenda. What would be the result of weakening or breaking down the unity of churches? Who is attempting to do this? What appears to be the desired end result of the disunity of the church? How would this change things? Who would benefit from this? How would this change the moral code of governing bodies? Does the source of this destruction appear to have an agenda? Is the source overlooking, ignoring, or leaving out information that doesn't support its agenda? Is the source using unnecessary influence to sway the people's perception of the facts? Where can you research using unbiased resources? What do different churches stand for? Why might the government be threatened by them? Who benefits from the strength and teachings of a church? Using credible sources, perform extensive and thorough research regarding this topic. Ask lots of questions, and seek as much information as possible without prejudice. Evaluate, analyze, and draw your own independent conclusions.

11. *Taking over the educational system.* It is not an accident that government sources have taken over and monopolized *control* over the public school system, and the *content* of information pushed onto the children and in universities. From the earliest stages of school life through college and even in advanced education, the government has taken over control of education. By brainwashing vulnerable people willing to learn and absorb the information presented from whom

they believe to be trusted sources, the political agenda has been advancing for generations. How are students in most educational systems being brainwashed and manipulated with an intentional agenda? What seems to be the reason for this happening? What appears to be the desired end results? How will this change things? Who does this benefit? Why was God taken out of the public school system? Why are political agendas inserted into them? What is the premise of controlling the responses students give? How are opinions of students being controlled by the educational system? How might capturing the minds of children in the early years of education benefit the agenda of those who control the system? Is unnecessary language being used for purposes of persuasion? Who is funding large universities? Is information being left out or deceptive? How can you find unbiased research regarding this topic? What do you think is going on? Utilize the research gathered and formulate your own unbiased and independent conclusions.

It is vitally important to critically think about ways manipulation can and will occur. There is no doubt that you are surrounded by propaganda and manipulation. Yet do not take my word for it. Do your own independent and unbiased research, and discover information from opposing sides. Formulate your own conclusions following adequate and thorough research. Find out where it takes you. Does any of it come as a surprise? What area has the greatest impact on you? Why do you think that is? What have you learned? How are you affected by this information?

Now that propaganda has been released like a "genie from a bottle," there is no "putting it back." How does the propaganda in social media affect you and your children, businesses, other groups, or organizations? How about Big Pharma and their new era of explicitly and carelessly promoting drugs and their agenda on all media sources now? Are you concerned with this advertising and subliminal messages, knowing the permission to deceive? How can you protect yourself from false or altered-truth information? Who benefits from this information? There are so many questions to be asked and information to be verified. Be careful as you navigate the muddy (and often polluted) waters of propaganda, and remember to critically think and perform extensive independent research before formulating conclusions.

> *The most effective way to destroy people is to deny and obliterate their own understanding of their history.*
>
> —George Orwell

> *Propaganda is to a democracy what the bludgeon is to a totalitarian state.*
>
> —Noam Chomsky

> *You can sway a thousand men by appealing to their prejudices quicker than you can convince one man by logic.*
>
> —Robert A. Heinlein

> *The whole aim of practical politics is to keep the population alarmed (and hence clamorous to be led to safety) by an endless series of hobgoblins, most of them imaginary.*
>
> —H. L. Mencken

> *Modern industrial civilization has developed within a certain system of convenient myths. The driving force of modern industrial civilization has been individual material gain, which is accepted as legitimate, even praiseworthy, on the grounds that private vices yield public benefits in the classic formulation.*
>
> *Now, it's long been understood very well that a society that is based on this principle will destroy itself in time. It can only persist with whatever suf-*

fering and injustice it entails as long as it's possible to pretend that the destructive forces that humans create are limited: that the world is an infinite garbage can. At this stage of history, either one of two things is possible: either the general population will take control of its own destiny and will concern itself with community interests, guided by values of solidarity and sympathy and concern for others; or, alternatively, there will be no destiny for anyone to control.

As long as some specialized class is in a position of authority, it is going to set policy in the special interests that it serves. But the conditions of survival, let alone justice, require rational social planning in the interests of the community as a whole and, by now, that means the global community. The question is whether privileged elites should dominate mass communication and should use this power as they tell us they must, namely, to impose necessary illusions, manipulate and deceive the stupid majority, and remove them from the public arena. The question, in brief, is whether democracy and freedom are values to be preserved or threats to be avoided. In this possibly terminal phase of human existence, democracy and freedom are more than values to be treasured, they may well be essential to survival.

—Noam Chomsky

 Reflect:

1. How have you noticed changes in propaganda through the past five years? Ten? Thirty?
2. How does propaganda affect you, your family, your career, or your business?

3. How could propaganda be used to benefit the American people? How about to the detriment of them?
4. What is your biggest concern regarding the current status of propaganda in all of the major media sources, Big Pharma, Big Tech, etc.?
5. How will you evaluate or research information you feel is concerning?
6. What other forms of manipulation can you add to the list included in this chapter? How would you critically think about the additional forms you came up with?
7. Read the books, references, cliff notes, or a summary, and the act mentioned in this chapter. How do you see a correlation to where we are today? What other titles can you think of that have the same source of information regarding this topic?

CHAPTER 8

What Happened in
Nineteen Eighty-Four?

We are coming to a time in the creation of our own history where there is a decision to be made between individuality and conformity. There is a battle between personal freedom and political repression. Faced with biased media outlets and additional forms of psychological intimidation, individual freedoms are becoming increasingly "challenged." George Orwell had astounding intuition or perhaps a *premonition*, as he wrote the infamous book *Nineteen Eighty-Four* in 1949.

Orwell's novel explored themes such as totalitarianism, communism, and a *dystopian* future.

> *A dystopia refers to a fictional place that is characterized by the universally miserable conditions under which its citizens live, usually under the guise of utopia.*[8]

In Orwell's setting, this fictional dystopia was created from war and government, with the main superstate, *Oceania*, in a constant state of war. The fictional dictator of *Oceania* is *Big Brother*, which is symbolic and designed to terrify the population into submission by those in power. This is the premise of the famous saying, "*Big Brother is watching you,*" which is in reference to the constant surveillance of the people.

The basis of the story revolves around the main character, Winston Smith, and his journey and struggle to gain individual freedom, which essentially never did happen. The novel also included a new language created by the government, *Newspeak,* with the intent to *suppress free thought.* Orwell realized the systems of communism and socialism would have difficulty succeeding when put into practice because the people in authority were generally greedy and *obsessed* with power and control. Orwell also wrote *Animal Farm* (1945). Along with *Nineteen Eighty-Four,* both novels blasted the totalitarian regimes and the control they seek over their citizens to basically turn them into submissive herds of sheep. Perhaps they can be thought of as "sheeple."

The novel continued with the mission to bring about change for the people that resembled Soviet Union communism and to *purge history* from the minds of the citizens. There are many more details and aspects of both *Nineteen Eight-Four* and *Animal Farm* that I encourage you to study for yourself. Take some time to read or listen to both of these novels written by George Orwell. Also, read numerous summaries and interpretations of each and compare and contrast these novels to the circumstances of our culture, society, and government today. Critically think about all aspects mentioned, including a dystopia, submission by fear, constant surveillance, suppression of speech and free thought, obsession with power and control, purging history, etc., so you can make logical and informed decisions to the best of your ability.

Who is doing what in the novels? Who is doing what in society? What seems to be the reason for this happening in the novels? What about in society? What are the end results of the novels? What are the desired or implied end results in society? How could these results change in either case? Does any of this concern you?

Your own independent research is key when comparing arguments, according to Will Erstad.[1] How will you independently verify the context or content? What sources will you use? How will you evaluate them? Develop an eye for unsourced claims so you can easily sort them out. Not all sources are equally valid. Learn the differences between them. Evaluate the information *objectively*, and be sure to evaluate *both* sides of the argument. Set aside your own personal bias so your judgment is not clouded. Identify the evidence that forms your beliefs, if possible.

What themes from both books parallel your society and culture today? Is there an attempt today to remove history from your mind? How about increasing conformity and promoting herd mentality, creating sheeple? There is a push for more reliance on the government as a type of utopia. Or is it actually, in reality, a *dystopia*? How about surveillance? Have you noticed that almost anyone, and everyone even, has access to your medical information?

Are your sources credible? In the evaluation of the information, who does the content benefit? Does the source appear to have an agenda? Does there appear to be any information excluded or overlooked? Is there bias or persuasion in the language? Assess the information and draw your own conclusion based on the data. Extrapolate and discover potential outcomes, understanding your inference will be made on the information collected, and additional information may lead to different conclusions. The more information gathered, the stronger the ability to formulate an educated conclusion.

What information is most relevant to your research? How will you determine relevance? What information are you seeking to discover? What is your end goal? These are all very important questions to ask as you collect raw data in your desire to come to your own educated and individually thought-out conclusion. Learn to think critically in all matters of importance. Draw your own conclusions and question the intent and content of others. Know your own reasonings and intentions, and seek to become fluent in critical thinking.

What are your thoughts about individuality versus conformity? What is the meaning of each of these words? Describe the way of life involved under each of these headings. Create different scenarios, and consider each label throughout each scenario. Who benefits from individuality? Who benefits from conformity? Picture yourself in a setting where everyone is their own person, choosing their own career, hobbies, activities, foods, and friends. Now visualize a setting where everyone is dressed the same, performing the same job, participating in the same hobby and activities, and eating the same food with the same people all presented to you without your selection. How would you feel about your ability to choose versus being presented with things *without* your choice? How would you benefit in either situation? How might you begin to lose yourself when your ability to choose is taken away? What is your ideal situation?

Have you ever wondered, especially recently, what it would be like to have free thought suppressed? How about free speech in the form of censorship, simply because you may not think the way someone else wants or expects you to? It's one thing if you are on the side of the one doing the suppressing, but what if you are the one being suppressed? Does this go against the freedom promised to you in the US Constitution? Does it ever appear that the news outlets treat you like part of the "herd," treating you like a sheep, expecting conformity and submission?

Allow yourself to continue to create a few more scenarios, comparing and contrasting the differences between individuality versus conformity. Be objective as you carefully consider each side. What research can you perform to learn more about the differences between the two? Where do your thoughts lead you regarding this exercise? Continue to observe the scenarios without prejudice by critically thinking about them and presenting yourself with lots of questions and extensive research. Draw your own conclusions after evaluating all of your research.

> *Every record has been destroyed or falsified, every book rewritten, every picture has been repainted, every statue and street building has been renamed, every date has been altered. And the process is continuing day by day and minute by minute. History has stopped. Nothing exists except an endless present in which Party is always right.*
>
> —George Orwell

Until they become conscious they will never rebel, and until after they have rebelled they cannot become conscious.

—George Orwell

Perhaps one did not want to be loved so much as to be understood.

—George Orwell

Now I will tell you the answer to my question. It is this. The Party seeks power entirely for its own sake. We are not interested in the good of others; we are interested solely in power, pure power. What pure power means you will understand presently. We are different from the oligarchies of the past in that we know what we are doing. All the others, even those who resembled ourselves, were cowards and hypocrites. The German Nazis and the Russian Communists came very close to us in their methods, but they never had the courage to recognize their own motives. They pretended, perhaps they even believed, that they had seized power unwillingly and for a limited time, and that just around the corner there lay a paradise where human beings would be free and equal. We are not like that. We know that no one ever seizes power with the intention of relinquishing it. Power is not a means; it's an end. One does not establish a dictatorship in order to safeguard a revolution; one makes the revolution in order to establish the dictatorship. The object of persecution is persecution. The object of torture is torture. The object of power is power. Now you begin to understand me.

—George Orwell

> *Being in a minority, even a minority of one, did not make you mad. There was truth and there was untruth, and if you clung to the truth even against the whole world, you were not mad.*
>
> —George Orwell

> *Big Brother is Watching You.*
>
> —George Orwell

> *Nothing was your own except the few cubic centimeters inside your mind.*
>
> —George Orwell

> *It was possible, no doubt, to imagine a society in which wealth, in the sense of personal possessions and luxuries, should be evenly distributed, while power remained in the hands of a small privileged caste. But in practice such a society could not long remain stable. For if leisure and security were enjoyed by all alike, the great mass of human beings who are normally stupefied by poverty would become literate and would learn to think for themselves; and when once they had done this, they would sooner or later realize that the privileged minority had no function, and they would sweep it away. In the long run, a hierarchical society was only possible on a basis of poverty and ignorance.*
>
> —George Orwell

 Reflect:

1. Read *Nineteen Eighty-Four* and *Animal Farm* by George Orwell. Summarize the key elements of each story. What conclusions do you draw?
2. How does each story compare and contrast the culture you live in today?

3. What sources did you use to evaluate? What information did you see as most relevant?
4. What is your biggest concern regarding the conclusions you came to? What is the premise of your concern?
5. How will you use this information in your daily life? How does it affect you?

CHAPTER 9

What Is Gaslighting?

Gaslighting "*is an insidious form of manipulation and psychological control.*"[9] All of the following content of description included here is derived from this same source. This chapter is intended to introduce the topic of gaslighting, bring awareness of its common occurrence, and place it under critical thinking scrutiny.

> *Victims of gaslighting are deliberately and systematically fed false information that leads them to question what they know to be true, often about themselves.*[9]

Has any news media outlet ever executed anything like this before? How about politicians or other people in authority? Is there anyone you currently know that has personally experienced this? Or maybe you know someone who actually *is* a gaslighter? Generally speaking, in gaslighting, the relationship starts well and may even involve praise or sharing confidences to build a trusted bond. The more quickly the victim becomes enamored, the quicker the next phase of manipulation typically begins.

The gaslighter then proceeds to lie about simple little things, followed by an increasing volume and content of lies, which continues to grow. If the victim questions the gaslighter, the victim may be accused of lying as a way to protect the strategy of the gaslighter.

Have *you* ever experienced this type of treatment? Have you seen it happen to someone dear to you? Did you recognize it as *gaslighting*, or did you not have a name for it then?

This type of treatment may become so intense and complex that the victim may end up *doubting their own memory, perception,* and even their *sanity*. It may even become difficult for them to see and recognize the truth. While the situation may start on a small level, the volume of misinformation may grow to be intense. Tactics are often employed to keep the victim engaged, such as showing some positive reinforcement in order to confuse the victim. Efforts may also be made to turn family and friends *against* this person by spreading lies to disassociate them from close bonds and create an "illusion of delusion."

The verbiage *gaslighting* originates from a 1938 British stage play and film adaptation, *Gas Light*. Victims of gaslighting *"are targeted at the core of their being: their sense of identity and self-worth."* [9] What groups can you think of that may be, or already have been, susceptible to becoming targets of gaslighting manipulation by targeting their identity and self-worth? How are they lured in? Who is attempting to lure them in? What seems to be the reason for gaslighting them? What are the desired end results of gaslighting them? What could this change? Who benefits from gaslighting someone? What is the premise of targeting these people? Is the source overlooking, ignoring, or leaving out information that doesn't support its agenda? Is the source using unnecessary, persuasive language to sway the victim's perception of the facts? The goal of this type of manipulation is to *attain power over* the victim through emotional, financial, or physical control.

What type of person is most susceptible to gaslighters?

1. Insecure
2. Lonely or alone, even a loner
3. Hurt or oppressed
4. Depressed or desperate
5. Involved in groupthink or herd mentality

6. Indecisive
7. Shy
8. Fearful or worrisome
9. Dependent
10. A follower mentality
11. Financially distraught
12. Circumstantially distraught
13. Mentally or physically distraught

Recognize the qualities mentioned as the *most likely* to fall prey to the guise of the gaslighter. The gaslighter will seek the most vulnerable, which are also the ones who will be *most easily* influenced. If you are in any of the categories mentioned previously, be aware of this possibility, and take extra precautions. Or better yet, develop an antidote to the mentioned issues and embark on a journey of self-improvement strategies to strengthen your confidence and increase your (already valuable) self-worth. More ideas can be found regarding further developing your own skill set in my book *Success is Ele-MENTAL*.

Gaslighters may be dictators, leaders, politicians, news media outlets, domestic abusers, bosses, narcissists, or cult leaders, to name a few. The most effective gaslighters may be hard to detect, being better recognized by the *damage induced upon* the victim and his or her actions and mental state.

> *Those who employ this tactic often have a personality disorder, narcissistic personality disorder, and psychopathy chief among them.*[9]

They are often seen by the world in one way and another by the victim. This also causes the victim concern for reaching out for help, fearing that they will not be believed. A gaslighter will typically repeat the behavior across several relationships. Keep in mind that gaslighters must have an *extreme* sense of insecurity, lack of compassion, and a mental disability, as they believe controlling you is the *only* way they can succeed with their agenda. Yet, they are also sly, cunning, shrewd, and immoral. This is a dangerous combination.

A primary objective of gaslighters is to keep the victim *hooked.* If doubted or disagreed with, gaslighters may try to make *themselves* the ones being victimized. Gaslighters may make promises of changing and other claims to keep the victim holding on, although as soon as the victim agrees to continue, things likely revert to how they were. Gaslighting can be psychologically devastating as it violates trust, alters the victim's view of people, and can make them suspicious of everyone close to them. A gaslighter also erodes a person's trust in themselves and causes them to forget what they once valued about themselves.

What is the difference between manipulation and gaslighting?

> *Manipulation is a key part of gaslighting, but manipulation is a fairly common tactic, and almost anyone is capable of employing it, while gaslighting, and gaslighters, are more rare.*

> *Gaslighting involves a pattern of abusive behaviors with the intent not just to influence someone, but to control them.*[9]

How has gaslighting crept into our society today? Do you see it in politics or news media outlets? How can you recognize when gaslighting is occurring? What might the agenda be for the one gaslighting? What could the underlying premise be? Who would benefit from gaslighting? What is deceitful in the approach of the source? How can you research to find more information? How can you decipher if a close friend or family member is a victim? What factors would you look for? How could you help someone in this unfortunate situation? How would you identify a perpetrator? What factors would you look for in this case? Where are likely places that this tactic might be employed? How can you prevent someone from taking advantage of you?

Considering all of the information presented about gaslighting, can you see how this is another way certain people seek to *take away freedom* from others? Precious freedom is under attack now more than ever in our society. As each freedom is relinquished, another entity, such as the government, becomes stronger. Dwell upon the fact that because we are "the home of the brave," we became "the land of the free." Apply critical thinking methods to what our fore-fathers *sacrificed* to provide us with the very freedom we now enjoy. What would happen if freedom gave way to conformity, and we were all *under the control* of the "conformist"?

Learn how to identify the characteristics of a gaslighter, as well as someone being abused by a gaslighter. Gaslighting is a cruel method of abusing the powers of influence and manipulation in order to *control* and *undermine* someone else—research many credible sources regarding this topic. Bring yourself to a clear understanding of what it is and how to easily identify when it is occurring. Take time to critically think about the factors involved with this disorder, and consider ways, based on your own conclusions, to guard against this immoral misuse of power.

> *Narcissists are consumed with maintaining a shallow false self to others. They're emotionally crippled souls that are addicted to attention. Because of this they use a multitude of games, in order to receive adoration. Sadly, they are the most ungodly of God's creations because they don't show remorse for their actions, take steps to make amends or have empathy for others. They are morally bankrupt.*
>
> —Shannon L. Alder

> *Gaslighting is mind control to make victims doubt their reality.*
>
> —Tracy Malone

> *I first came across the term gaslighting in the context of abusive romantic partners, but it shows up in larger-scale relationships, too, like those between bosses and their employees, politicians and their supporters, spiritual leaders and their devotees.*

Across the board, gaslighting is a way of psychologically manipulating someone (or many people) such that they doubt their own reality, as a way to gain and maintain control.

—Amanda Montell

In terms of gaslighting, I define it as "to implant false and/or distorted narratives that are specifically designed or formulated to manipulate a person into a destructive web of deception, loss of control, and the surrender of personal freedom and beliefs of self-worth, self-value, self-esteem, and productivity."

—Ross Rosenberg

Gaslighting is a subtle form of emotional manipulation that often results in the recipient doubting their own perception of reality and their sanity. In addition, gaslighting is a method of manipulation by toxic people to gain power over you. The worst part about gaslighting is that it undermines your self-worth to the point where you're second-guessing everything.

—Dana Arcuri

 Reflect:

1. Define the term *gaslighting*. How would you identify the characteristics of someone being abused by a gaslighter? How would you identify and define a perpetrator?
2. How has gaslighting affected you personally? Your family? Your career or business?
3. How has gaslighting made its way into the political sector?
4. What is your biggest concern regarding gaslighting in positions of high authority?

5. How will you evaluate or research information, without prejudice, that you feel is concerning regarding gaslighting? How can you become better informed based on your own research?

CHAPTER 10

Why Censor?

Censorship is the suppression of speech, public communication, or other information.

Political censorship exists when a government attempts to conceal, fake, distort, or falsify information that its citizens receive by suppressing or crowding out political news that the public might receive through news outlets.

People are unable to dissent from the government or political party in charge in the absence of neutral or objective information. This is something they count on.

> *This term also extends to the systematic suppression of views that are contrary to those of the government in power. The government often possesses the power of the army and the secret police, to enforce the compliance of journalists with the will of the authorities to spread the story that the ruling authorities want the people to believe. At times this involves bribery, defamation, imprisonment, and even assassination.*[10]

There are many different forms of censorship found in many different arenas. Even self-censorship is sometimes used by authors, artists, inventors, etc., to protect their artistic work. It is important not only to be aware that censorship exists but also to be able to critically think through each case of censorship you may encounter. You need to be able to draw your own conclusions based on logic and sound reasoning backed by evidence and raw data. Lacking the ability to think critically could be detrimental to your ability to come to a truth-based conclusion. You must possess the ability to analyze information effectively and without prejudice.

Your freedoms in society today are disappearing faster than at any other time in history. There is risk at hand if you do not learn to think more critically. There is a greater chance that you will succumb to fraud, manipulation, gaslighting, propaganda, etc., if you cannot think critically. Is there any evidence of censorship that you see in society today? Analyze the issue of censorship and all facts, data, and evidence related to it. The challenge is to do so without the influence of personal feelings, opinions, or biases. Analyze based on factual information only.

Once again, go back to the act passed in 2013, permitting and encouraging false, deceptive, and mis- or disinformation in propaganda. As mentioned earlier, having read or listened to this, you now know that the censorship by the major news and social media outlets is *not* due to any form of misinformation since this was approved in 2013. Simply put, censorship is *fear*. Fear that others will find out. Therefore, what are they afraid of? *What* don't they want *you* to know? The truth? Why are they censoring some of the most intelligent and talented people in the world for speaking out about what they personally witnessed in their fields of expertise? Any form of censorship, other than personal censorship to protect your own artistic work, should raise a flag of alert and make you desire to seek additional information, including extensive research regarding opposing views of the topic at hand. Censorship is based on an *insecurity* of the one doing the censoring. It is a fear of someone revealing something that the *"censor"* doesn't want others to know. This should *always* make you begin the process of critical thinking.

Who is doing the censoring? What seems to be the reason for the censoring? What appears to be the desired end result of it? How could this change things? Who does the censoring benefit? Does the source of censoring appear to have an agenda? Are they emotionally driven? Is the source of the censoring overlooking, ignoring, or leaving out information that doesn't support its beliefs or claims? Is the source of the censoring using unnecessary language to sway an audience's perception of a fact?

Remember, your ability to *independently research* is key to having authenticity. Verify your sources of information and evaluate them within your own means. If sources you discover are *not* willing to expose where the information came from, let that be a red flag to you. Verify your sources. If possible, evaluate claims from both sides of an argument, being aware of possible biases from either or both sides. Practice setting aside your own personal biases, as this will most likely cloud your judgment. Learn to see things from alternate vantage points.

Do you identify censorship in the news media outlets today? How about social media? How about in the entertainment industry? What about in the government or politics in general? How about on a local level within your community? Where else do you see censorship occurring? Have you ever censored anyone from anything? Has anyone ever censored you personally? Critically think about the reasons behind each of the scenarios mentioned. Ask objective and unbiased questions. Always select the most important and relevant information regarding the topic—in this case, censorship. Determine what establishes clear direction in what you are trying to figure out. What is your end goal? Once you have gathered and collected the most relevant material, assess the information and draw your own conclusions based on the unbiased data. This is such an important skill in mastering the art of critical thinking. What have you concluded about censorship? How do you see it in your surrounding environment? Be aware of the occurrences, and critically think in each case.

> *Censorship is to art as lynching is to justice.*
> —Henry Louis Gates Jr.

> *Whoever would overthrow the liberty of a*
> *nation must begin by subduing the freeness of speech.*
> —Benjamin Franklin

Let us be clear: censorship is cowardice. It masks corruption. It is a school of torture: it teaches, and accustoms one to the use of force against an idea, to submit thought to an alien "other." But worst still, censorship destroys criticism, which is the essential ingredient of culture.

—Pablo Antonio Cuadra

Once a government is committed to the principle of silencing the voice of opposition, it has only one way to go, and that is down the path of increasingly repressive measures, until it becomes a source of terror to all its citizens and creates a country where everyone lives in fear.

—Harry S. Truman

Think for yourselves and let others enjoy the privilege to do so, too.

—Voltaire

 Reflect:

1. Where do you notice censorship in the world today?
2. Summarize the key elements of the censorship. What conclusions do you draw?
3. How does the idea of censorship compare and contrast to the culture you live in today?
4. What sources did you use to evaluate the censorship? What information did you see as most relevant?
5. What is your biggest concern regarding the conclusions you came to regarding censorship? What is the premise of your concern?
6. How will you use this information in your daily life? How does it affect you?

CHAPTER 11

Why Cancel?

Cancel culture, also known as call-out culture, is a phrase contemporary to the late two thousand tens to two thousand twentys used to refer to a culture in which those who are deemed to have acted or spoken in an unacceptable manner are ostracized, boycotted or shunned. This shunning may extend to social or professional circles—whether on social media or in person—with most high-profile incidents involving celebrities. Those subject to this ostracism are said to have been "canceled."[11]

Canceling can also be in the form of *publicly shaming* a person or group of people. It could also mean withdrawing support for some form of public figure or company based on something they did or said that was found to be in some way *offensive* or objectionable. It is a form of rejection that potentially denies someone the right to apologize or somehow resolve a mistake that may have been made. Whether a mistake or simply being objectionable, the possibility of being *called out* exists within the terms of the *cancel culture*.

Canceling also stems from issues of *insecurity* and a deep-seated *need for control*. It is a version of "stomping your feet" to get your way and denying someone the right to their opinion or freedom of speech. Apply the same measures of critical thinking to the issues involving cancel culture. What is the source of information? Where did it come from? Was it independently verified? How do you evaluate the source of information? How about the content of the information? What is the reliability of the source and the content? Do you fully understand the information collected? What additional resources have been used for interpretation?

What is the premise of the argument for canceling? Who stands to benefit from it? Who is doing what regarding canceling? What seems to be the goal or end result of the canceling? How could this change things? What was the position of the one being canceled? What appeared to be the premise? Evaluate the claims on both sides of the argument. View things from differing points of view. Does the source of canceling appear to have an agenda? Are they overlooking or intentionally leaving out information that opposes their claim? Are they using unnecessary language to sway the audience to their cancel?

Assess the information regarding the canceling issue independently, extrapolating and discovering potential outcomes. Make a conscious effort to remain unbiased and use only relevant information based on confirmed and trusted sources. Using logical reasoning based on factual information, what do you think is going on?

How is canceling linked to conformity? Is it yet another method to snatch away your freedom? How do you perceive it in relation to a form of control? Realize the ones who do the canceling are the ones who are afraid, insecure, and trying to bully their way to power and control. They do not want you to think for yourself and especially express your own opinion if it differs from theirs. Understanding the source and the reasoning allows you to see more clearly when this is happening, by whom, and why.

Continue to utilize the same methods of critical thinking presented in this book. Train yourself to analyze situations using an array of relevant, factual, and unbiased sources, looking at them from opposing perspectives. Is the process of critical thinking becoming easier? Have you noticed yourself asking the same form of questions almost instinctively yet? Take the time to program this information into your mind so you become *automatically* programmed to think critically and instinctively regarding all matters.

> *In a cancel culture, we appoint ourselves the arbiters of right and wrong and also the judge and jury, because thanks to social media, we get to dole out punishment.*
>
> —Unknown

> *Cancel culture is not actually about justice. It is about control. People use cancellation to force conformity to ideals.*
>
> —Teal Swan

> *Cancel culture is a pretentious form of bullying.*
>
> —Unknown

> *Cancel culture is a term bounced around by people afraid of accountability. But freedom of speech does not mean freedom from consequences.*
>
> —Monisha Rajesh

> *Cancel culture grows because we accept (and gluttonously consume) social violence. We no longer seek truth or both sides of a story. Whichever side is loudest, wins...regardless of its relationship to the truth.*
>
> —Steve Maraboli

> *We live in a generation of emotionally weak people. Everything has to be watered down because it's offensive, including the truth.*
>
> —Unknown

 Reflect:

1. Where do you notice cancel culture in the world today? How does it affect you?
2. Summarize the key elements of the cancel culture. What information do you draw from this?
3. How does the idea of cancel culture compare and contrast to the culture you live in today?
4. What sources did you use to evaluate the cancel culture? What information do you see as most relevant?
5. What is your biggest concern regarding your conclusions about cancel culture today? What is the premise of your concern?

CHAPTER 12

Conclusion

After much discussion and review of a vast amount of ideas, thoughts, stories, and concepts, what have *you* concluded regarding *Who Connects Your Dots?* Did you determine whether or not *other* news media sources have taken on this role and taken over the connection for you? What about the Internet with the World Wide Web? Social media? Or did you determine that *you* actually are in control of critical thinking and connecting your own dots by utilizing your *own* sound analysis and evaluation? Are there any changes or alterations you need or would like to make? Where will you be applying critical thinking methods? Who else could benefit from gaining an understanding of this process?

It is both fascinating and concerning to think about how many sources and which ones have programmed your mind since the day you were born. If not addressed, these other influences could continue to be the reason why you respond as you do, sometimes challenging your very own values. Has the presented information caused you to think about the current programming of your mind? In my previous book, *Elevate Your Mind to Success,* I lay the foundation for the basis of the preprogrammed mind and provide detailed thoughts, ideas, and suggestions on how to acknowledge your current programming, then remove, replace, and reframe your thoughts to align with your current design of values and beliefs. This ties in with the focused and pragmatic ability to critically think, especially regarding sensitive or controversial matters. You must know who you are and what you believe in, in order to properly reprogram your mind to *instinctively* respond in ways that are *supportively* aligned with your values.

Be *on the lookout* for bias in the world that surrounds you. You will find that it is *everywhere* you look. It is tempting to succumb to the strategically *offensive* biases and respond with a just-as-emotional, *defensive* reply. However, this could only further escalate the topic or situation at hand, flaring additional emotions in a senseless tizzy, all while defying logical thought. Take a step back, or maybe even two, and engage your *powerfully* effective critical-thinking skills in an unprejudiced effort to draw on verified, extrapolated, and factual data, leading to logical insight.

In previous chapters, we discussed a few of the many ways your freedom is being snatched from you in plain sight. Some of these sources include biased major media outlets, erasing your history, and brainwashing found in the educational school system, to name a few. It is important to be aware of how and why these things are happening. The rate of progression for these changes is astounding, and you can be certain this movement will continue and expand as it does. Learn how to discover unbiased yet factual research material and methods, and do your own analysis and evaluation. Use your critical-thinking skills to evaluate opposing sides to bring more enlightenment to your analysis. Awareness is always the first step in any situation. Start to understand what and why things are progressing the way they are. The key here is to ascertain this information independently and free from prejudice.

The book continues by defining the vital method of critical thinking, the basis for this important action, and how to perform it properly. It is imperative to bring yourself to a complete understanding of the methods and particulars of thinking in this manner. Critical thinking is a skill that *must* be practiced and mastered in order to contend with this vastly changing culture. Taking an unbiased stance is necessary to comprehend *all* aspects of the situation and develop insight from *all* perspectives. Just as with the success of the Trojan horse in the city of Troy, there is always more clarity and a better position when you have access to the opposing side's most vulnerable information. In addition, as more knowledge is gained, more doors may open with possibilities of an altered opinion or way of doing things. Always be open to the possibility of absorbing new information that may lead to a fresh perspective you may have been previously unaware of. You may discover missing pieces to a story that change your entire perspective. If you are not open to the possibility, you may be supporting something unintentional or unfavorable to your true beliefs.

The Milgram experiments, performed by Stanley Milgram, were brought forth and discussed, revealing human behavior regarding obedience while under authority. From these experiments, we learned that ordinary people likely follow orders from an authority figure for one of many reasons, even to the extent of killing innocent human beings. Obedience to authority is ingrained in people to the degree that it has been preprogrammed into their minds. People are capable of acting as *agents* for another person's will. Along with the guise of authority, many other factors are influential in persuading decision-making in people, which were discussed in previous chapters. Be aware of these factors and how people can be easily influenced by others to do unethical or even unexplainable things while under their misguided pretenses.

Critical-thinking methods were implored and practiced on a series of thought-provoking topics, including for potential reasons of feeling a need to identify and the common and growing stance today of placing blame on others rather than taking responsibility or being accountable for actions of self. Both of these topics have appeared to *grow wings* of their own and have *taken flight*. A source of this focus has been through the use of numerous sources of propaganda. Propaganda was defined, along with its intention to control how you think and act. Propaganda relies on manipulation, and keys to successful manipulation were explored and discussed for thinking application. Discussion ensued regarding the book *Nineteen Eighty-Four* to exemplify the ingenious "premonition" of George Orwell regarding the potential result of manipulation, control, and brainwashing of people by authority figures with a self-serving agenda.

And finally, gaslighting, censorship, and cancel culture were defined and processed through the critical-thinking method. Critical thinking is more important and vital than *ever* before. Being skillfully adapted to this process helps awaken and potentially *immunize* you to the negative effects of manipulation, persuasion, and influence of powerful governing bodies that surround you, at least to a certain extent. It takes dedication, hard work, and a concentrated effort to master critical thinking skills. *Who Connects Your Dots?* has broken down the basic elements of critical thinking and has offered ideas, suggestions, examples, and questions to hone your skills in order to become a better and even instinctual critical thinker. By performing these skills, you will use logic to make informed, factual, and unbiased decisions, giving you an edge on your individuality and strength in your freedom against conformity.

> *The third-rate mind is only happy when it is thinking with the majority. A second-rate mind is only happy when it is thinking with the minority. A first-rate mind is only happy when it is thinking.*
> —A. A. Milne

> *The important thing is not to stop questioning. Curiosity has its own reason for existing.*
> —Albert Einstein

> *It is a mark of an educated mind to be able to entertain a thought without accepting it.*
> —Aristotle

> *Critical thinking is not something you do once with an issue and then drop it. It requires that we update our knowledge as new information comes in.*
> —Daniel Levitin

The essence of the independent mind lies not in what it thinks, but in how it thinks.
—Christopher Hitchens

Freethinkers are those who are willing to use their minds without prejudice and without fearing to understand things that clash with their own customs, privileges, or beliefs. This state of mind is not common, but it is essential for critical thinking.
—Leo Tolstoy

To think incisively and to think for one's self is very difficult. We are prone to let our mental lives become invaded by legions of half-truths, prejudices, and propaganda. At this point, I wonder whether or not education is fulfilling its purpose. A great majority of the so-called educated people do not think logically and scientifically. Even the press, the classroom, the platforms, and the pulpit in many instances do not give us objective and unbiased truths. To save man from the morass of propaganda, in my opinion, is one of the chief aims of education. Education must enable one to sift and weigh evidence, to discern the true from the false, the real from the unreal, and the facts from the fiction. The function of education, therefore, is to teach one to think intensively and to think critically.
—Dr. Martin Luther King Jr.

 Reflect:

1. Define the skill of critical thinking. Summarize the key elements of it. How will you apply these particular skills in your daily life?

2. How will you word questions so they are framed in an unbiased manner? Make a list of questions you will ask yourself when you employ the process of critical thinking.
3. What sources will you use to educate yourself further on critical thinking? How will you choose the sources? How will you validate the integrity of the sources?
4. What is your biggest insight or concern about the conclusions you came to regarding the manipulation that surrounds you? What is the premise of your concern?
5. How has this information impacted the way you think?
6. How will you apply the information you learned from this book to your daily life?
7. Who will you share this information with?

CRITICAL THINKING
QUESTIONS

To discover the truth, you must first ask the right questions.
—Jill Fandrich

Who is doing what?
What seems to be the reason for this happening?
What appears to be the desired end results?
How could they change?
What are the surrounding circumstances?
Whom does this benefit?
How does this affect you?
Does the source of this information appear to have an agenda?
What is the agenda?
Does the message have a bias?
Is the source overlooking, ignoring, or leaving out information that doesn't support its beliefs or claims?
Is there censoring involved for opposing views?
If so, why would this be?
Is the source using unnecessary or persuasive language to sway an audience's perception of a fact?
Is their funding involved?
Who is funding the source?
Is there a financial incentive involved?
How could this affect decisions?
How can you find reliable and credible resources?
How can you verify their credibility?
Is the information sourced or unsourced?

Is anything else being hidden?
What information is most relevant?
What other critical thoughts come to mind?
What do you think is going on?

Create Your Own Questions

1.

2.

3.

4.

5.

———————

JOURNAL

Great thinkers are *note*-worthy.

—Jill Fandrich

Date:
Topic:

"How could I have applied critical thinking to my interactions today?"

"What mistakes did I make?"

"How can I do it differently next time?"

"Where could I improve?"

"What did I do right?"

"What have I learned from this experience?"

Other questions?

JOURNAL

Great thinkers are *note*-worthy.

—Jill Fandrich

Date:
Topic:

"How could I have applied critical thinking to my interactions today?"

"What mistakes did I make?"

"How can I do it differently next time?"

"Where could I improve?"

"What did I do right?"

"What have I learned from this experience?"

Other questions?

JOURNAL

Great thinkers are *note*-worthy.

—Jill Fandrich

Date:
Topic:

"How could I have applied critical thinking to my interactions today?"

"What mistakes did I make?"

"How can I do it differently next time?"

"Where could I improve?"

"What did I do right?"

"What have I learned from this experience?"

Other questions?

JOURNAL

Great thinkers are *note*-worthy.

—Jill Fandrich

Date:
Topic:

"How could I have applied critical thinking to my interactions today?"

"What mistakes did I make?"

"How can I do it differently next time?"

"Where could I improve?"

"What did I do right?"

"What have I learned from this experience?"

Other questions?

JOURNAL

Great thinkers are *note*-worthy.

—Jill Fandrich

Date:
Topic:

"How could I have applied critical thinking to my interactions today?"

"What mistakes did I make?"

"How can I do it differently next time?"

"Where could I improve?"

"What did I do right?"

"What have I learned from this experience?"

Other questions?

JOURNAL

Great thinkers are *note*-worthy.

—Jill Fandrich

Date:
Topic:

"How could I have applied critical thinking to my interactions today?"

"What mistakes did I make?"

"How can I do it differently next time?"

"Where could I improve?"

"What did I do right?"

"What have I learned from this experience?"

Other questions?

JOURNAL

Great thinkers are *note*-worthy.

—Jill Fandrich

Date:
Topic:

"How could I have applied critical thinking to my interactions today?"

"What mistakes did I make?"

"How can I do it differently next time?"

"Where could I improve?"

"What did I do right?"

"What have I learned from this experience?"

Other questions?

ENDNOTES

1   Will Erstad, "6 Critical Thinking Skills You Need to Master Now," January 22, 2018, accessed January 24, 2023, https://www.rasmussen.edu/student-experience/college-life/critical-thinking-skills-to-master-now/.

2   "Turtles All the Way Down: Vaccine Science and Myth," https://tinyurl.com/TurtlesBookEngRef.

3   "Milgram Experiment," Wikipedia, accessed January 28, 2023, https://en.m.wikipedia.org/wiki/Milgram_experiment.

4   Edward Bernays, Propaganda (Ig Publishing, 2005).

5   John Hudson, "U.S. Repeals Propaganda Ban, Spreads Government-Made News to Americans," July 14, 2013, accessed March 15, 2023, https://foreignpolicy.com/2013/07/14/u-s-repeals-propaganda-ban-spreads-government-made-news-to-Americans/.

6   "Turtles All the Way Down," https://tinyurl.com/TurtlesBookChap1Eng.

7   "Died Suddenly 2022 (Full Documentary)," accessed March 15, 2023, https://rumble.com/v1wcs7o-died-suddenly-2022-full-documentary.html.

8   Liz Breazeale and Jenna Clayton, "When Was 1984 Written?" Study.com, December 2, 2021, accessed February 2, 2023, https://study.com/academy/lesson/when-was-1984-written.html.

9   "Gaslighting," Psychology Today, 2023, accessed January 30, 2023, https://www.psychologytoday.com/us/basics/gaslighting.

10 "Censorship," Wikipedia, 2023, accessed January 30, 2023, https://en.m.wikipedia.org/wiki/Censorship.

11 "Cancel Culture," Wikipedia, 2023, accessed January 3, 2023, https://en.m.wikipedis.org/wiki/Cancel_culture.

ABOUT THE AUTHOR

Jill Fandrich, PharmD, received her doctorate in pharmacy from Shenandoah University in Winchester, Virginia, and her degrees in chemistry and pharmacy from Westminster College and the University of Pittsburgh, respectively. During this time, she was a noted and accomplished public speaker, presenter and educator, diabetes care specialist, writer, artist, performer, director of pharmacy, and media personality with a passion for helping people to feel and live their best.

As an entrepreneur, Jill simultaneously became integrated into other endeavors of improving her community with house restoration and built corporations in the real estate and financial sectors, participating with other local entrepreneurs and businesses in joint cooperation of beautification.

Jill has most recently focused on her passion for writing to guide and encourage people and empower them to develop and discover their own unique and full potential. She is the author of *Elevate Your Mind to Success, Success is Ele-MENTAL, COVID-19 Prevention,*

Parents: COVID-19 Prevention for Kids, and is a book reviewer and author of "A Book in Time Blog" found at www.ABookinTime.net, where she educates, inspires, motivates, and energizes people to utilize their own unique skills and abilities to bring about the leader and success potential already located from within.

When not writing, Jill can be found spending time with friends and family; traveling; golfing; trading currencies; reading; running; walking; playing tennis; fixing, remodeling, or building things; being actively involved with her church; gardening; air frying; or just puzzling on one of her hand-built puzzle boards.

Jill was born and raised in St. Marys, Pennsylvania, and has spent the majority of her life in Florida. She is currently residing in Fort Myers, Florida, where she continues to passionately write full-time regarding success strategies, leadership development, positive mind transformation, critical thinking, and young adult, teen, and adult fiction novels.